Beyond the Hotline

Beyond

How Crisis Control Can

edited by Martin Linsky

BOSTON

the Hotline

Prevent Nuclear War

William L. Ury

HOUGHTON MIFFLIN COMPANY
1985

Library of Congress Cataloging in Publication Data

Ury, William.
Beyond the hotline.
Bibliography: p.
Includes index.
1. Nuclear crisis control—United States. 2. Nuclear
crisis control—Soviet Union. I. Linsky, Martin.
II. Title.
JX1974.8.U78 1985 327.1'74 84-25131
ISBN 0-395-36671-2

Printed in the United States of America

V 10 9 8 7 6 5 4 3 2 1

To my mother,
Janice Gray Ury,
crisis controller *extraordinaire*

"The greatest danger of war seems to me not to be in the deliberate actions of wicked men, but in the inability of harassed men to manage events that have run away with them."

HENRY KISSINGER

"There is no longer any such thing as strategy, only crisis management."

ROBERT S. MCNAMARA

Contents

Preface

In September 1982, the United States Arms Control and Disarmament Agency asked the Harvard Negotiation Project to apply its ideas to an extraordinarily difficult and critical negotiation: that which would take place between the United States and the Soviet Union in an acute crisis. How can such a crisis best be controlled or, even better, headed off before it begins?

A new project was born to examine the question. The Nuclear Negotiation Project, based at Harvard Law School, issued its report in March 1984, concluding that "crisis control offers one of the most significant opportunities today to reduce the risk of nuclear war."

Despite its promise, however, crisis control is not yet widely recognized by the public. The report and other writings on the subject are addressed to a specialized audience in government and academia. Many ordinary citizens, however, faced with the numbing statistics and horrifying images of the nuclear danger, have been looking for a practical and constructive approach to which they themselves might contribute. This book argues that crisis control is one such approach and offers a brief introduction to the subject for the general reader.

This is not a scholarly book. But the subject of crisis control is rich in technical subtleties, and the history of every superpower crisis is rife with scholarly disputes over what actually happened. Perhaps the hardest task in writing this book, then, was conveying the ideas as clearly and readably as possible without unduly oversimplifying. Where I have not succeeded in properly describing the complexity of a particular point, I apologize to any of my academic colleagues who may be offended. The original report to the government is intended for them.

My greatest debt in writing this book is owed to Richard Smoke, co-author with me of the report. He shared equally in the conception and development of the ideas expressed in the report and in this book. I am deeply grateful for his collaboration.

Two years ago, Roger Fisher inspired the initiation of the research project and helped me understand the anatomy of crisis. More than twenty years ago, Thomas Schelling built much of the intellectual foundation on which the book stands. His incisive criticism of early versions of its ideas has left them much stronger.

I have benefited immensely from the comments of those who read earlier versions of the manuscript. I am thankful to Graham Allison, Steve Boyd, Dan Caldwell, Giuseppe Ciallelli, Gisela DeDomenico, Mark Garrison, Chellis Glendinning, James Goodwin, Fen Hampson, François Leydet, Judith Merrill, Joseph Nye, Alex Randall, John Ratcliffe, Wendy Roberts, Steve Rothstein, Scott Sagan, Larry Smith, Greg Treverton, Rick Williamson, and Shari Young. Bob McKersie deserves special thanks for painstakingly reading two drafts, as does Ronnie Heifetz for patiently listening with a sensitive ear to the book being read aloud.

Bruce Allyn, with great thoroughness and acumen, researched the Soviet perspective described in chapter 9. Craig Kennedy, with assistance from Dan Abbasi, applied a fine scholarly talent to tracking down and checking out countless factual sources. Webster Stone provided the intriguing account of the history of the Hotline and hunted down the photographs with unsurpassed initiative. All four pored over the manuscript, giving invaluable editorial and substantive advice.

Without Ellen Meyer and Ruth Sparrow, her assistant, there might be no book. They supervised every detail of production, ably keeping successive crises under control, as well as commenting perceptively on each draft. Bob DeMarais patiently coaxed the word processor into turning out draft after draft. Marc Sarkady sensitively harmonized a lengthy and demanding process.

Special thanks go to the institutions that made this work possible: the U.S. Arms Control and Disarmament Agency, which funded the original research project; the Avoiding Nuclear War Project at Harvard's John F. Kennedy School of Government, funded by the Carnegie Corporation; the Ploughshares Fund, which supported some additional research; Peace and Common Security of San Francisco, funded in part by the Columbia Foundation; and the Program on Negotiation at Harvard Law School.

Without friends, writing would be an intolerable task. Dave Lax and Jim Sebenius supported me at every turn with advice and good company. I owe more than I can say to Lynn Ciallelli's love and warm encouragement.

My agent, Rafe Sagalyn, espoused the book early on, gave valuable substantive advice, and, rarest of all, backed it with genuine passion. I am also grateful to Robie Macauley and his colleagues at Houghton Mifflin for their patience and devotion to quality.

Finally, there is Martin Linsky, who put enormous effort and talent into organizing, editing, and cutting the manuscript. His contributions were so great that he can properly be acknowledged only on the title page.

W.L.U.

Cambridge, Massachusetts
September 1984

Beyond the Hotline

Prologue: The Silver Trumpets

In the days of King Arthur, Mordred, the king's son, rebelled and raised an army to overthrow his father. Two great hosts of knights met on the field of Camlan, but at the last moment father and son decided not to fight. Instead they called a truce and sent spokesmen forward to seek an agreement. Meanwhile, each army, suspecting a trick, stood poised for battle.

Negotiations were proceeding smoothly until a snake, slithering in the grass, suddenly bit one of the knights. The knight cried out and drew his sword to kill it. The assembled armies mistook this as a general signal for battle and sprang to the attack. By day's end, all but two of the one hundred thousand warriors lay dead. King Arthur and his son fought and killed each other, and with them perished Camelot, forever.

Today the nations of the West and the nations of the East face a similar danger. Each side has marshaled enormous military forces poised to strike at any moment. Fearing total mutual destruction, the two sides have been talking — but gingerly, suspiciously, and sometimes very little. An uneasy truce has lasted almost forty years. Yet, at any time, a regional conflict, a terrorist act, or an accident could suddenly ignite a deadly confrontation between the superpowers.

If we could rewrite the legend of Arthur and Mordred, we might choose to give father and son each a silver trumpet so that they could have blown them to signal their armies that a mistake had been made and that no battle was intended. A simple pair of trumpets would have permitted the peace talks to continue. Eventually the armies might have disbanded and Camelot might have survived.

Today the United States and the Soviet Union, and their allies around the world, need the equivalent of those silver trumpets. That is the subject of this book.

Why Crisis Control?

Every man, woman and child lives under a nuclear sword of Damocles, hanging by the slenderest of threads, capable of being cut at any moment by accident or miscalculation or madness . . . Unless man can match his strides in weaponry and technology with equal strides in social and political development, our great strength, like that of the dinosaur, will become incapable of proper control, and man, like the dinosaur, will vanish from the earth.

President John F. Kennedy
United Nations address
25 September 1961

We live in a world of crises. Every morning the newspaper — and every evening the newscast — confronts us with the latest trouble spot. One day the focus is on Central America. The next it is the Middle East. Then Africa. There are military skirmishes, coups and countercoups, guerrilla activities, terrorist attacks, and border tensions all around the globe. Often American and Soviet forces stand nearby, lending a hand to opposing sides.

These crises in themselves provide cause for great concern, often taking a terrible toll in human suffering. Yet the anxiety and fear they arouse run even deeper. To many, they seem like brush fires raging in different spots around the world, never very far from a highly combustible conflict between the United States and the Soviet Union with their huge nuclear arsenals. A single spark conceivably could start a fire that, if allowed to burn out of control, might ultimately become an inferno that destroys our societies. The likelihood may be small, but the potential consequences are so devastating that the strongest preventive measures are called for.

While the deadly possibilities are well known, the potential solutions seem far more limited. To some, there appears to be no way out over the long run. Even to those who believe there may be a way, the task may seem too large and difficult for a single individual or small group to make a difference.

This book grapples with the questions: Is there a way out? Is there some way to begin to regain the control we appear to have lost over our collective and individual destinies? And is there some constructive way an individual can channel his concern into practical action? This book discusses the approach of crisis control: improving the ability of nations to halt crises before they become wars, and, better still, to prevent crises from erupting in the first place. Crisis control offers one of the most promising opportunities today to reduce the risk of nuclear war.

To explain the significance of this approach requires returning to the question of how a nuclear war between the superpowers could ever come about. On first thought, it seems inconceivable. No leader in his right mind would deliberately launch a nuclear attack, because it would only provoke a devastating retaliation. It would be tantamount to national suicide.

Unfortunately, however, there exists another path to war. It receives less attention than does the danger of a deliberate attack, but it is real nonetheless — perhaps even more so. It is the path of miscalculation in time of intense crisis, of miscommunication, of human blunders and organizational foul-ups. It is the path not of cool calculation but of runaway escalation. It is the path by which the kingdom of Camelot came to its bloody end.

This is what happened in the summer of 1914. On June 28 Archduke Franz Ferdinand, heir apparent to the Austrian throne, was assassinated in the sleepy provincial town of Sarajevo. The murder, a tragic but comparatively minor incident, nonetheless ignited a European crisis. No leader wanted a world war. Throughout the month of July, each tried to prevent it or at least to limit it. But through a combination of miscalculations, misunderstandings, and rigidly laid plans, the crisis escalated out of control by August into a war that continued for four years and decimated a generation of young Europeans.

The danger has continued into the nuclear age. During the Cuban missile crisis in October 1962, both President John F. Kennedy and Premier Nikita Khrushchev were desperately anxious to avoid war, yet each was conscious of how all too easily the situation could slip out of their control. Kennedy calculated, rightly or wrongly, the odds of war at "somewhere between one out of three and even." Khrushchev described the crisis as a time "when the smell of burning hung in the air." He pleaded with Kennedy not to pull any tighter on "the knot of war."

What makes a crisis so treacherous? Most crises, including U.S.-Soviet confrontations, are ignited by the spark of some sudden event. As in July 1914 or October 1962, decision makers are quickly compelled to make life-and-death decisions with little time to decide, a dangerously high level of uncertainty, and few usable options to choose from. Under these conditions, even the most rational decision makers can miscalculate or miscommunicate. One human error often triggers another. A hasty decision to escalate in order to protect one's interests may provoke a similar escalation by the other side, which in turn impels the first side to escalate still further. A point may soon be reached in this action-reaction cycle when the decision makers simply lose control and war breaks out.

This is the process of runaway escalation. It may be the most likely path to nuclear war. At its heart is the human factor — the propensity to make mistakes in time of intense crisis. Against this no number of weapons, no threat of retaliation, can offer protection. Deterrence assumes that the other side will decide rationally. It may not work against nonrational and irrational behavior by people and organizations.

For decades, policy on both sides has focused on the danger of *deliberate* attacks. An immense body of doctrines and a huge catalogue of weapons systems are geared to this threat. Military leaders, architects of foreign policy, even presidents, are trained and encouraged to think in these terms. Yet unintended war, which receives far less attention, may now be the greater danger.

Until now, most efforts to prevent war have focused on the nuclear weapons themselves. Should we freeze them? Should we reduce them? Should we even increase them? Yet arms reductions, while vital in their own right, cannot alone stop war by human error. Cutting by half the number of knights on the field of Camlan would not have prevented the fatal clash. Cutting by half the fifty thousand nuclear weapons currently in the two arsenals would not save us if war broke out. A few hundred could destroy American society. It may take only a few thousand to end human civilization. While pursuing reductions, then, we need to ensure that the weapons that exist are never used. But how?

One way to think about this question is to imagine yourself in the shoes of the president of the United States on the day a new Middle East war broke out or when a nuclear missile was launched by accident. What might you wish you had talked about beforehand with your Soviet counterpart? What agreements to halt escalation would you wish you had reached? What procedures would you want to have in place to ensure you were able either to defuse the crisis or, better yet, prevent it in the first place? These steps must be taken ahead of time, because once a crisis erupts it may be too late to create new procedures.

A system to control nuclear crises would loosely resemble all the other "crisis control systems" that surround us every day and protect us from fires, floods, airplane crashes, and medical emergencies. Consider the fire prevention system. Until quite recently, fire was the great fear of humanity. In a few minutes, a fire raging out of control could destroy everything — one's house, one's crops, and sometimes one's life. Cities, with their closely placed buildings, posed the worst danger. When Mrs. O'Leary's cow kicked over a lantern in 1871, it began a fire that consumed most of Chicago. Today cities are more densely populated and filled with explosive materials than ever before. But thanks to fire stations and fire hydrants, emergency exits and smoke detectors, building regulations and fire drills in school, trained firefighters and their modern equipment — in short, a comprehensive fire prevention and firefighting system — we live in relative safety.

The same approach can be taken with crises. Like fires, crises are endemic; some are accidental, others are caused deliberately. In either case, they can be effectively stopped before they go out of control. For instance, a joint U.S.-Soviet crisis control center — half in Washington, half in Moscow, linked by instant teleconferencing — could monitor possible dangers and stand ready to help defuse a crisis on a moment's notice. The two sides could agree on standard procedures to keep a spark from being ignited when their worldwide forces come in contact with each other. Other nations around the world and international organizations such as the United Nations could strengthen their capabilities to undertake crisis mediation and neutral peacekeeping in order to keep regional conflicts from drawing in the superpowers. The president and his advisers could receive a detailed briefing, just before entering office, on what is known about controlling crises. Such institutions and procedures would be central elements of a crisis control system.

Can such a system work between nations that are in deep-seated conflict with each other? In some ways, it already does. Every even hour on the hour, an American officer in the Pentagon sends a message on the Hotline to his Soviet counterpart in Moscow; every odd hour on the hour, he receives a message back. Continually tested, the Hotline comes into use during times of high tension. The president and the Soviet premier communicate directly to defuse crises, as they already have, for example, over the Middle East war of 1967 and the Lebanon crisis of 1982.

Consider, too, that around the world, at each moment of the day, Soviet and American naval vessels and planes are following each other, sometimes coming dangerously close. In the late 1960s and early 1970s, this practice led to numerous collisions and near-misses. Since 1972, however, with the signing of the Incidents at Sea Agreement, these "close encounters" have drastically decreased. Captains in both navies have special rule books that tell them how to communicate and avoid accidents. Every six months, in times of high tension as well as in more normal times, officers from both navies meet to review the process.

The Hotline and the Incidents at Sea Agreement are two initial building blocks of a crisis control system. Learning from their success, we can create a full-fledged system to prevent runaway escalation.

Such steps are politically feasible. Both the superpowers want to eliminate the risk of unintended war; and crisis control does not evoke the fears of military inferiority that stymie the arms talks. The time is right, too; interest is growing. In June 1984 the United States Senate voted 82 to 0 for a resolution, originally offered by Senators Sam Nunn of Georgia and John Warner of Virginia, urging the president to propose a crisis control center to the Soviets. Shortly thereafter, both nations agreed to improve the Hotline, allowing it to transmit pages of information almost instantaneously.

If history is any guide, however, the creation of a system will require a great deal more. The Hotline was proposed in the late 1950s and viewed with favor by both sides. But it might not have become reality when it did, had it not been for two things: the persistence of a maverick magazine editor and the occurrence of the Cuban missile crisis. For three straight years, the editor of *Parade* magazine, Jess Gorkin, carried on a public campaign for the Hotline; thousands of his readers joined him. They successfully helped put the Hotline high on the national and international political agenda. Even so, it took the shock of the Cuban missile crisis to create the political will and sense of urgency for the superpowers to finally agree to the direct link.

In the domain of fire safety, too, almost every existing measure has come into being only *after* a major disaster. But in the nuclear age, nations cannot afford to learn the hard way. Each close call like the Cuban missile crisis is one too many.

How can the requisite political will be generated? Government interest alone is not enough. Ultimately support must spring from the individual citizen. Crisis control will require the concerted efforts of many kinds of people — private citizen and government official, media professional and member of Congress, Soviet and American, European and Third World citizen. Far from being a powerless spectator, the individual may hold the key to success.

Hence this book, intended as a general introduction to crisis control for those interested in a practical approach to which they themselves might contribute. *Beyond the Hotline* does three things. Part I explores the danger of unintended war. What are the possible sparks? What makes crises so dangerously hard to control? Part II goes on to sketch out how the basic elements of a crisis control system would work to eliminate sparks and keep those small fires that do start under tight control. Part II also grapples with the hard case: What if the other side wants to win the crisis, not defuse it? Part III answers the question of what happens next. What about crisis control in the Kremlin — will the Soviets agree? And what about the Americans? This last part suggests some practical ideas for citizens who want to translate their desire to prevent nuclear war into effective action.

This book is not about "command, control, communication, and intelligence" (or c^3i), the technical term for unilateral measures to improve control over one's nuclear forces. Admittedly, though, each side's c^3i systems are extremely important to its ability to control crises. Nor is this book about traditional "confidence-building measures," such as agreements by NATO and the Warsaw Pact nations to exchange observers during troop movements. Instead, this book focuses on new measures the United States, the Soviet Union, and other nations can take *together* to prevent and stop crises.

Crisis control is in no way a substitute for arms reductions, improved relations, or deterrence. It is an essential complement to all three, a systematic handling of the human factor. It deals with the most likely way war might occur. It is practical and politically feasible. Comparatively little has been done so far. For all these reasons, crisis control offers great promise as a means of reducing the nuclear danger.

Whether you favor the nuclear freeze or oppose it, whether you believe in peace through strength or peace through disarmament, whether you believe you can act constructively or despair of the ineffectiveness of action, crisis control should be of keen interest. Because it is common sense, crisis control is common ground.

PART I

The Most Likely Path to War

1

Sparks in the Tinderbox

> [The] role [of the Berlin crisis] may be compared to a smoldering fuse connected to a powder keg. Incidents arising here, even if they seem to be of local significance, may, in an atmosphere of heated passions, suspicion, and mutual apprehensions, cause a conflagration which will be difficult to extinguish.
>
> *Pravda*
> 28 November 1958

Five times in recent history, the United States and the Soviet Union have come uncomfortably close to nuclear war: Berlin in 1948 and in 1961, Cuba in 1962, and most recently in the Middle East wars of 1967 and 1973. During each crisis, a mistake or miscalculation at a crucial moment could conceivably have sparked the ultimate escalation.

June 1948. The Soviet Union blocks off all overland access from the Western zone of Germany to West Berlin. Moscow wants to force the American, British, and French occupying troops to leave Berlin. The British foreign secretary declares that "the abandonment of Berlin would mean the loss of Western Europe." For President Harry S Truman, there is no wavering. "We are going to stay, period."

The Western powers seriously consider pushing their way through with an armed convoy but opt instead for a temporary airlift of food and coal to the two and a quarter million people in West Berlin. The planes fly one behind another, morning, noon, and night. The Soviets try to disrupt the airlift by "buzzing" the incoming planes and provoking near collisions. They turn powerful searchlights on Western pilots flying in at night, trying to blind them.

The people of West Berlin begin to protest in the streets. At one demonstration at the Soviet war memorial in the British sector, the Russian guards open fire, killing several people and wounding others. Only quick action by the British provost marshal to stop the firing and to disperse the crowd prevents the situation from escalating further into open fighting between troops.

On July 21, General Lucius Clay, the American commander, tells Secretary of Defense James Forrestal that "the chances of war are about one in four." Even the Soviets, who downplay the risks, later will write of how the world in 1948 stood "at the brink of war." In mid-September, President Truman makes a private decision to use nuclear weapons "if necessary."

Eventually, in the face of Western determination, the Soviets lift the blockade.

June 1961. The underlying conflict over Berlin continues, another major crisis having erupted in 1958. Now yet another is at hand. Premier Khrushchev announces that he will sign a separate peace treaty with East Germany by the end of the year. He demands that the Western allies withdraw their forces from Berlin. East Germans flee in increasing numbers to the Western zone. Tensions rise. In August, East Germany cuts off access between the two zones and begins building the Berlin Wall. Fleeing refugees are shot, American planes are harassed, and troops of each side move to the borders.

In late October, the crisis reaches a climax. When the East

German police deny entry to Alan Lightner, deputy chief of the U.S. mission in Berlin (on the grounds that he is not wearing a military uniform), presidential envoy General Lucius Clay orders several tanks and armored personnel carriers to Checkpoint Charlie. With this show of force plus an armed escort of eight soldiers with fixed bayonets, Lightner enters East Berlin without inspection. Five days later, American tanks appear again at Checkpoint Charlie to force uninspected entry. The Soviets respond with seven T-54 tanks. They move forward, guns aimed at the American tanks, stopping within a hundred yards of the barrier. The American tanks move closer. More American tanks arrive, followed by more Soviet tanks. For the first time in the cold war, Soviet and American forces confront each other, weapons poised.

At the crucial moment, however, the United States decides not to force uninspected entry of Western personnel, and the next day the Soviets withdraw their tanks. The United States follows suit. American diplomats continue to enter Berlin without inspection.

October 1962. It is October 27, the "Black Saturday" of the Cuban missile crisis. The Soviet ships carrying their cargo of missiles keep coming toward the naval quarantine. Employees of the Soviet consulate in New York shred records in anticipation of the possibility of war. Kennedy's advisers have decided earlier that if an American U-2 is downed over Cuba, the United States will retaliate with a strike against an antiaircraft missile site. The air force is ready. Then it happens. An American U-2 is shot down; the pilot is killed. President Kennedy sees the incident as putting the superpowers "in an entirely new ball game." Secretary of Defense Robert S. McNamara looks at the spectacular sunset that evening and wonders how many more sunsets he will see.

But Kennedy hesitates. He decides not to retaliate, at least

US ARMY CHECKPOINT
YOU ARE
THE AMERIC
ВЫ ВЫЕЗ
АМЕРИКАНСК
VOUS S
DU SECTEUR
10

not yet. Instead he increases diplomatic pressure on Khrushchev. The next day Khrushchev sends word that he will withdraw the missiles. War is averted.

June 1967. War breaks out in the Middle East. The Israelis rapidly begin winning. On June 10, Premier Aleksei Kosygin sends a message to President Lyndon Johnson on the Hotline. The Soviets have been supporting Syria with large shipments of military equipment and substantial numbers of advisers. They are concerned the Israelis will attack Damascus. In Johnson's words, "Kosygin said a 'very crucial moment' had now arrived. He spoke of the possibility of 'independent decision' by Moscow. He foresaw the risk of a 'grave catastrophe' and stated that unless Israel unconditionally halted operations within the next few hours, the Soviet Union would take 'necessary actions, including military.' "

Johnson orders the Sixth Fleet to draw closer to the Syrian coast, signaling American resolve to resist by force any Soviet intrusion into the war. He sends a message to Kosygin that Syria and Israel are close to a cease-fire agreement. He tells Kosygin that the United States has been pressing Israel to make the cease-fire effective and has received assurances that this will be done. Later that morning Israel and Syria do move toward a cease-fire, and there is no military action by the superpowers.

October 1973. It is near the end of the next major Middle East war. The Israelis surround the Egyptian Third Army and threaten to destroy it, which would humiliate Egypt and deal

OPPOSITE: **Checkpoint Charlie.** October 1961: In Berlin, American and Soviet armor face each other for more than sixteen hours at a two-hundred-yard range. As President Truman put it, "A hotheaded Communist tank commander might create an incident that could ignite the powder keg." (AP/Wide World Photos)

a severe blow to the credibility of Egypt's patron, the Soviet Union. Denouncing Israel, the Soviets warn the United States that the "gravest consequences" will ensue from a continued Israeli advance. They prepare to enter the war. Soviet leader Leonid Brezhnev sends President Richard Nixon a message: "I will say it straight, that if you find it impossible to act together with us in this matter, we should be faced with the necessity urgently to consider the question of taking appropriate steps unilaterally." The American leadership meets. Within an hour they order American forces all over the world, both conventional and nuclear, to go on alert. Nixon responds to Brezhnev, warning of the "incalculable consequences" Soviet intervention would bring.

Finally, under intense American pressure, the Israelis acquiesce. They do not capture the Third Army. The Soviets decide not to intervene. And again, the crisis subsides.

On each of these five occasions when the United States and the Soviet Union have neared the brink, it has been through an escalating crisis in which neither side intended to go to war. Each time both sides made efforts in the very midst of the crisis to avoid war. Even when pursuing its own objectives and exacerbating the crisis, each side showed significant restraint. But each time, a series of miscalculations, miscommunications, accidents, or other unexpected events could conceivably have sent the crisis spiraling out of control.

We Live in a Tinderbox

All five nuclear crises have arisen in trouble spots. The world is full of them. Many of the conflicts in such areas have the potential to escalate and to involve the superpowers in a confrontation neither side intends. The Soviet description of Berlin in 1958 as "a smoldering fuse connected to a powder keg" could have applied just as well to Lebanon in 1983. Many feel the same fear when they read about each new international crisis: that somewhere hidden in it are the seeds of nuclear war.

In the first three of these crises — Berlin 1948, Berlin 1961, and Cuba 1962 — the Soviets intentionally took some action that challenged the United States. Direct confrontations deliberately started by one side are one kind of spark that could ignite a nuclear confrontation. Significantly, no potentially nuclear crisis just like this has occurred for more than two decades, but another is certainly possible.

In the two most recent of these crises, both in the Middle East, the unintended factor was strongly present. Both escalated out of regional conflicts in which the superpowers were indirectly involved. Neither Moscow nor Washington initially sought to challenge the other. They were drawn in despite their original intention to stay out. It is the unintended factor that seems to be the slowly growing danger now.

Even in the three earlier crises, the unintended factor was present in some respects. Perhaps the chief danger in the Berlin riots of 1948, the Checkpoint Charlie incident in 1961, and the naval quarantine of Cuba in 1962 was that some sailor, border guard, or local commander would do something the national leadership did not want. Fighting would begin and the crisis would escape the control of decision makers in Washington and Moscow. As President Truman put it at the time of the 1948 Berlin crisis, "A trigger-happy Russian pilot or hotheaded Communist tank commander might create an incident that could ignite the powder keg."

In the Middle East wars of 1967 and 1973, the unintended factor was there from the beginning. In each case, neither superpower wanted the war. Once it began, however, American and Soviet interests in the region came into play, in direct competition with each other. The United States resupplied

Israel with huge arms shipments, and the USSR did the same for Egypt and Syria.

But even then, the main risk of nuclear war lay in developments that Washington and Moscow did not anticipate. For instance, Washington did not intend that Israel win either war so completely that Damascus would be overrun (1967) or that the whole Egyptian Third Army would be destroyed (1973). Such results would have placed Moscow in an intolerable position. When those possibilities unexpectedly materialized, Washington tried to restrain Israel — successfully, as it turned out.

With their excessive risk of runaway escalation, these Middle East wars are warning signs for the future. Perhaps the greatest danger of global war lies in an unintended nuclear confrontation sparked off either by a close encounter between superpower forces, a regional crisis, or perhaps a freak nuclear detonation.

Close Encounters

One unintended risk in the Middle East wars stemmed from accidental contacts between American and Soviet forces. Both sides had navies in the eastern Mediterranean. It is not inconceivable that a spark from the regional brush fire could have ignited a superpower naval battle. Indeed, there was a possible spark.

At one point during the 1967 war, Israeli planes and gunboats attacked a U.S. communications ship, the *Liberty,* off the coast of Syria. Washington soon learned of the attack, but as President Johnson recalled, "For seventy tense minutes we had no idea who was responsible." The Soviets' intentions were unclear. U.S. Secretary of Defense Robert McNamara "thought the *Liberty* had been attacked by Soviet forces."

Johnson ordered carrier planes to investigate, and sent

Moscow a message on the Hotline explaining this action and giving assurances that the United States was not about to intervene in the war. An hour later, when the Israelis discovered they had made a tragic mistake, their apology to Washington was also passed along on the Hotline. McNamara later remarked, "Thank goodness our carrier commanders did not launch immediately against the Soviet ships who were operating in the Mediterranean."

American and Soviet forces operate in close proximity not just in times and places of crisis such as the 1967 war in the Middle East but at all times, all around the globe. Both navies patrol the same seas, and their planes constantly pass in the skies. Dangerous incidents do occur. In November 1969, for instance, the U.S. nuclear submarine *Gato* collided with a Soviet nuclear submarine at the entrance to the White Sea. According to a United Press International account of a secret congressional report, the *Gato* prepared for action with nuclear torpedoes, but the Soviet crew was so confused about what had been hit that the Americans were able to steal away. More recently, in March 1984, a Soviet submarine collided with the American aircraft carrier *Kitty Hawk* in the Sea of Japan.

So far, no nuclear crisis has ensued from such a close encounter. But suppose such an incident took place in a moment of great Soviet-American tension? At the height of the Cuban missile crisis, an American military reconnaissance plane on a mission from Alaska to the North Pole inadvertently strayed over Siberia. Soviet fighters scrambled to intercept it. The pilot radioed for help and American fighters in Alaska took off to escort him home. Fortunately, no dogfight took place. When he learned the news, President Kennedy, who thought he had canceled all routine flights near the Soviet Union, exclaimed, "There's always some son of a bitch who doesn't get the word."

Another kind of risk stems from the proximity, and routine interaction, of American and Soviet strategic nuclear systems. When Soviet submarines approach the shores of the United States — as they regularly do — aircraft engines are started at nearby American bomber bases. When such suspicious events occur, the computerized warning and command systems on each side do not just ring bells; they automatically cause actions to be taken. Urgent messages are sent out, bombers and submarines are ordered to change their positions, and other steps are taken that the equally automatic warning systems on the other side can observe. This information in turn can trigger this warning system to order similar military actions automatically, which of course are noticed and responded to immediately by the first side's system. In a time of crisis, when forces are on alert, this back-and-forth process could ratchet upward: It may be easier for the process to keep going than to stop. Safeguards exist, of course, but some danger remains and in fact tends to grow over time as the systems become more tightly coupled and the flight times of missiles become shorter.

Regional Conflicts

On almost any day, several wars are being fought in the Third World. Others are on the verge of erupting. In many cases, the forces of the superpowers are not far off, in part because American and Soviet leaders hold the view that their countries' national interests extend over much of the world, if only to counter the influence and strategic position of the other side.

Although the scope of their interests is not diminishing, the superpowers do not have as much influence as they once had. World economic, political, and military power is becoming more diffuse. In many regional conflicts, the superpowers are less able to sway their respective clients. The growth of international terrorism adds yet another wild card. The stage is thus set for a new superpower crisis that, as in 1967 or 1973, could escalate overnight out of a regional conflict but that may be more difficult than ever to control.

In addition, a special danger is brewing. As time passes, the possibility grows that some Third World nation will use a nuclear weapon. Israel has nuclear weapons, or can assemble them from stockpiled components on a moment's notice. India has a nuclear weapons capability, and Pakistan and South Africa are not too far from it. Other candidates for the nuclear club include South Korea, Argentina, and Taiwan. Iran and Libya tend to arouse the most fear as nations who might wield nuclear weapons if they had them. Libya sought unsuccessfully to buy a bomb from China in 1974, offering $2 billion. Fortunately, the Chinese refused. But will all potential suppliers always refuse to sell?

If nuclear weapons are used in a regional conflict such as that in the Middle East, or between India and Pakistan, devastating escalation could follow. Imagine that a new Middle East war breaks out. This time, a radical Palestinian group announces that it has secreted nuclear bombs in Haifa and Tel Aviv. The bombs are hidden well below ground so they cannot be found by search teams with radiation detectors. The radicals insist that Israel end the war on Arab terms and accept a Palestinian state. Israel threatens nuclear retaliation against all its Arab enemies if the bombs are detonated. The Soviets quickly counterthreaten complete nuclear devastation of Israel if Israel strikes. The United States calls a worldwide strategic alert and warns the Soviets not to intervene. The radicals give Israel a four-hour ultimatum to meet their demands or the first bomb will be detonated. What then?

Freak Detonations

The ever-evolving development of nuclear weapons and the spread of nuclear know-how has created another source of possible sparks. Several avenues are opening up through which just one or perhaps several nuclear weapons might strike the United States, the Soviet Union, or their respective European allies.

One, just mentioned in the Middle East scenario, is nuclear terrorism. Although the obstacles are great, it is not impossible that a terrorist group could obtain an atomic bomb through theft, manufacture, or acquisition from a country such as Colonel Muammar al-Qaddafi's Libya. A number of well-known novels and films are based on this theme. In the best-selling book *The Fifth Horseman,* terrorists sponsored by Qaddafi plant a nuclear bomb in New York City, threatening to explode it unless the United States compels Israel to withdraw to its original 1967 borders.

The danger of nuclear terrorism is hardly imaginary. In 1974 the Boston police received a nuclear terrorist threat credible enough to take seriously and inform the president. Helicopters flew over the city with Geiger counters, trying to detect a nuclear device. Nothing was found and nothing occurred, then or a few years later when a similar threat was received in Los Angeles. But when will a real threat occur?

A dangerous variation on nuclear terrorism is an agent provocateur attack. Suppose the "mad" leader of a state, believing his nation would be better off without the superpowers, exploded a nuclear device first in a ship in New York Harbor, then shortly thereafter in one off Vladivostok, hoping thereby to trigger a nuclear exchange?

The possibility that such an attack could be pulled off successfully is remote but nonetheless real. Agent provocateur attacks have taken place at other times in other places.

During World War II, for instance, the German air force bombed the Hungarian city of Kassa with Russian bombs in order to make the Hungarians think they were being attacked by the Soviets. The ruse was successful: The Hungarians examined the bomb fragments, discovered them to be of Russian manufacture, and declared war on the Soviet Union.

A freak detonation need not be set off by a third party. There always exists a tiny but appreciable danger that a nuclear weapon could be set off by technical accident. Richard Nixon recalls that when he visited Russia as vice-president, Nikita Khrushchev "told me of a Soviet missile firing . . . which headed, completely by mistake, toward Alaska." A couple of years later, in 1961, an American B-52 bomber was forced to jettison a twenty-four-megaton nuclear bomb over Goldsboro, North Carolina. Although the bomb apparently lacked its nuclear "capsule," it was disturbing that of the six interlocking safety devices, five were set off by the fall.

Since these events and others, both the United States and the USSR have instituted substantial fail-safe systems and procedures. Still, the possibility cannot be ignored altogether, particularly as American and Soviet nuclear weapons systems become more numerous and more complex. As Paul Bracken, a specialist in command and control systems, notes, "The complexity of the system has made us safer from accidental war [but] it protects us only against the discrete, isolated failure. Multiple errors or malfunctions are a different matter altogether . . . The problem with compound accidents . . . is that the number of possible reactions is enormous and no design can protect against all of them."

An unauthorized launch is not impossible either. The movie *Dr. Strangelove* depicted a commander of a remote bomber base suddenly breaking under the strain and sending off his bombers. There are careful safeguards against this happening, but the possibility cannot be ruled out, especially on submarines, where the officers have more discretion, and during conditions of tension and nuclear alert, when some of the safeguards may be removed.

Madness is not the only problem, however; the dangers of misunderstood instructions and misguided judgment are probably more serious. Paul Bracken quotes an interview from the early 1960s that a defense specialist conducted with the American commander of a small air base in Korea with ten nuclear bombers. Asked about his instructions for launching the planes, he answered: "It's the oldest principle of war that a commander has the right and authority to protect his troops. If I thought my troops were in danger, for example if I heard of . . . an explosion, somewhere else in the Pacific during an alert, I would send them off."

"And what do you think they would do?"

"If they did not get an execute order, I think they'd come back . . . Of course, if one of them broke out of that circle and headed for his target, I think the others would follow, and they might as well," he added philosophically, "because if they go, we might as well all go."

A Growing Danger

Close encounters, regional conflicts, and freak detonations are three general sources of possible sparks. Within these categories one can imagine countless scenarios that could conceivably lead to an intense Soviet-American confrontation, and perhaps to a nuclear war. Any particular path to unintended nuclear war may be extremely unlikely, but if all the potential paths are added up, the cumulative risk is impossible to ignore.

Perhaps the most worrisome danger is the possibility of several events occurring at about the same time, interacting to produce effects none of them could by itself. A coincidence of unexpected events and accidents could occur, for example, at a moment of acute U.S.-Soviet tension. Paul Bracken describes one such instance that took place in 1956, just at the time that the Hungarians were revolting, the British and French were trying to take the Suez Canal back from Egypt, and the Soviets were threatening to destroy London and Paris with nuclear missiles:

> The headquarters of the U.S. military command in Europe received a flash message that unidentified jet aircraft were flying over Turkey and that the Turkish air force had gone on alert in response. There were additional reports of 100 Soviet MiG-15s over Syria and further reports that a British Canberra bomber had been shot down also over Syria. (In the mid-1950s only the Soviet MiGs had the ability to shoot down the high-flying Canberras.) Finally, there were reports that a Russian fleet was moving through the Dardanelles . . . The White House reaction to these events is not fully known, but reportedly General Andrew Goodpaster was afraid that the events "might trigger off all the NATO operations plan." At this time, the NATO operations plan called for all-out nuclear strikes on the Soviet Union.
>
> As it turned out, the "jets" over Turkey were actually a flock of swans picked up on radar and incorrectly identified, and the 100 Soviet MiGs over Syria were really a much smaller routine escort returning the president of Syria from a state visit to Moscow. The British Canberra bomber was downed by mechanical difficulty, and the Soviet fleet was engaging in a long-scheduled exercise.

If this coincidence had been suggested as a "scenario," it would have been dismissed as too improbable to take seriously. Yet it actually occurred. What coincidences, seemingly improbable, could occur today? The most dangerous scenario may be the one no one foresees.

This is not to suggest that such perilous interactions are likely, but simply that we do not really know. No one fully understands why complex systems, even those designed with multiple safeguards, break down. The nuclear reactor accident at Three Mile Island in 1979 is a case in point. Considered by many experts beforehand to be almost impossible, it nevertheless took place with potentially disastrous consequences. With the stakes infinitely higher in a nuclear confrontation and the level of knowledge about the system perhaps even lower, it seems only prudent while we seek long-term solutions to the nuclear dilemma to institute the best safety system possible.

To conclude, the growing menace of unintended war has profound implications for U.S. and Soviet policy. It highlights the powerful interest both superpowers share in preventing the runaway escalation of a crisis. As the unintended factor grows in crises, so does this shared interest and so does the need for crisis control.

2

Runaway Escalation

It isn't the first step that concerns me, but both sides escalating to the fourth and fifth step — and we don't go to the sixth, because there is no one around to do so.

John F. Kennedy,
during the Cuban
missile crisis

Knowing how to halt runaway escalation before it turns into a nuclear war requires knowing first how things get out of control. How do thoughtful, prudent national leaders get caught up in a spiral of escalation that in the end produces a war neither side desired? What is the treacherous quality of crises that causes seemingly rational decision making to lead to an irrational outcome?

Intuitively, we all know a crisis when we see one. There is great tension and a sense of imminent threat. But that alone is not enough to create so perverse an outcome as an unintended war. If we could understand what makes a crisis a crisis, we could perhaps grasp its special danger. In 1914, for instance, an isolated incident in Sarajevo triggered a crisis that eventually resulted in a devastating world war, despite almost universal intentions on the part of the great nations

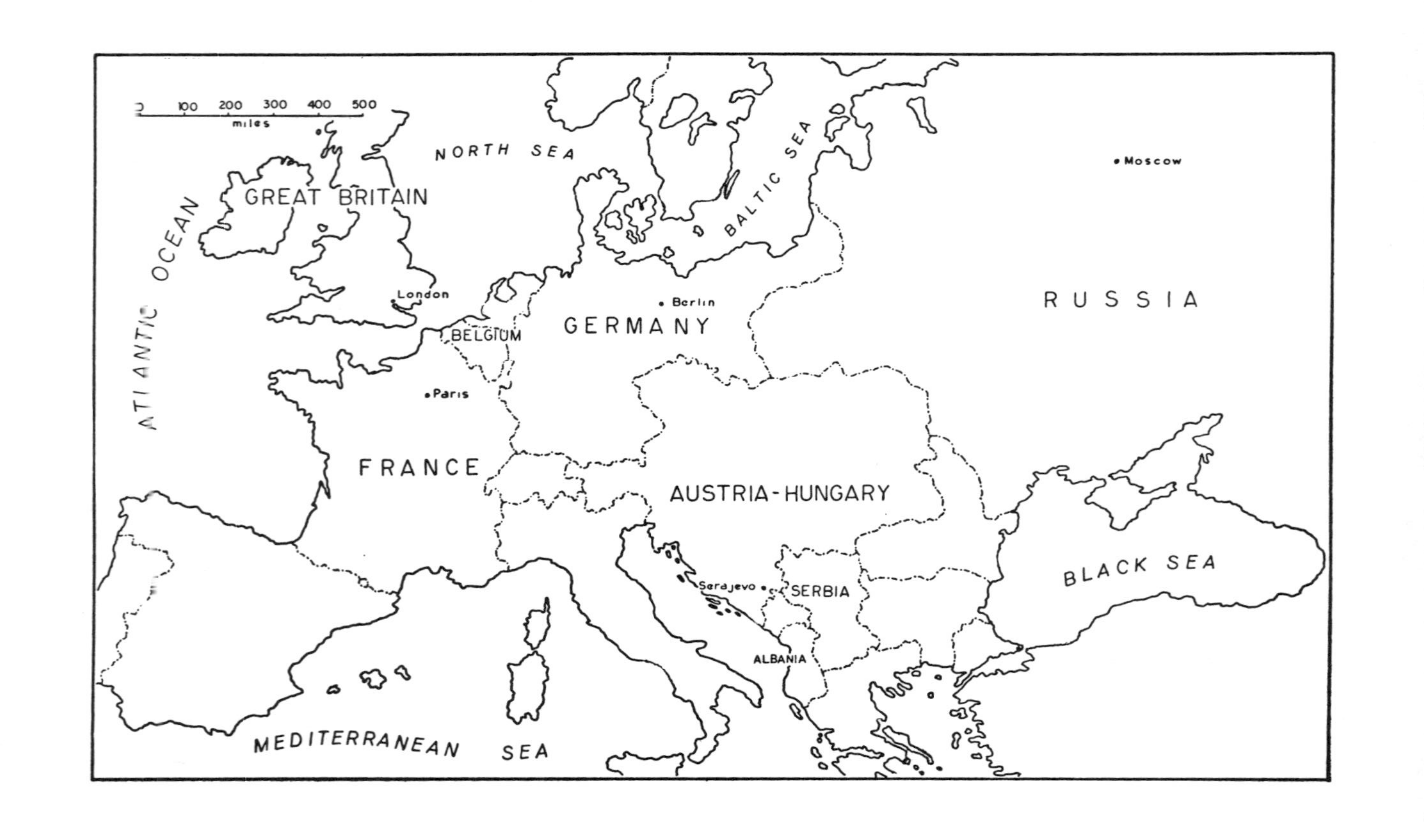
0 100 200 300 400 500
miles
NORTH SEA
BALTIC SEA
Moscow
GREAT BRITAIN
ATLANTIC OCEAN
London
Berlin
RUSSIA
GERMANY
BELGIUM
Paris
FRANCE
AUSTRIA-HUNGARY
BLACK SEA
Serajevo
SERBIA
ALBANIA
MEDITERRANEAN SEA

of Europe to keep the conflict limited. How could that have happened?

It was late June of that year when a young Serbian nationalist assassinated Archduke Franz Ferdinand, heir apparent to the throne of Austria-Hungary. By mid-July, Emperor Franz Josef, his uncle, presented Serbia with a harsh ultimatum. When Serbia failed to comply by July 28, Austria-Hungary declared war on the small Slavic country. Tsar Nicholas II of Russia appeared to have only two options: to mobilize against Austria-Hungary so as to deter her, or to do nothing. If he mobilized, there would be a chance that he might have to go to war against Austria-Hungary and, worse yet, against Germany, its powerful ally. He did not want such a war. His forces were not prepared. Yet if he did not act quickly, Austria-Hungary would invade Serbia, his ally, and annex it with impunity. He would look foolish and weak, no longer deserving the status of a Great Power.

On July 30, the tsar ordered a general Russian mobilization. Then, uncertain of the consequences and fearful of war, he canceled the order. He tried to limit the mobilization to one clearly directed against Austria-Hungary, but his generals convinced him that there were insurmountable technical difficulties in executing a partial mobilization. So, having floundered into mobilization, the next day the tsar reversed his reversal and reordered the general mobilization, despite both his own serious misgivings and, more ominously, German warnings.

The next day, Germany issued an ultimatum demanding a cessation of Russian preparations on the German border.

OPPOSITE: **Europe on the Verge of War. July 1914.** "An isolated incident in Sarajevo triggered a crisis that eventually resulted in a devastating world war, despite almost universal intentions on the part of the great nations of Europe to keep the conflict limited."

Then, without receiving a reply from Russia, Germany mobilized and declared war.

For his part, Kaiser Wilhelm II of Germany was also somewhat unenthusiastic about a war, particularly if it threatened to involve Great Britain as well. At one point, he had the idea that the affair between Serbia and Austria-Hungary could be solved by mediation. He went around with this notion in his head for three days. The Russians had offered peace several days before, having already mobilized against Austria-Hungary. But Wilhelm misread the communication from the tsar.

In the early hours of the morning of July 30, he wrote in the margin of the message from the tsar, ". . . I cannot agree to any more mediation, since the tsar who requested it has at the same time secretly mobilized behind my back. It is only a maneuver, in order to hold us back and to increase the start they have already got. My work is at an end!" Later, the kaiser added, "In view of the colossal war preparations of Russia now discovered, this is all too late, I fear. Begin! Now!"

As it became apparent, however, that the British were serious about joining the war on the side of the Russians, the German leaders began to have second thoughts. On August 1, having given General Helmuth von Moltke permission to mobilize, the kaiser called him back to stop mobilization against France. "Your majesty," von Moltke replied, "it cannot be done [You will not have] an army ready for battle, but a disorganized mob of armed men."

So Germany went ahead with the mobilization. On August 3, it declared war against France, and the next day, Britain declared war against Germany. Within a few weeks, a crisis sparked by an assassination, a local Balkan dispute, had escalated out of control into a general European war that eventually would spread to a large part of the world. When the war ended, the Austro-Hungarian Empire had dissolved, the tsar was dead, a victim of the Russian Revolution, and the kaiser had lost his throne. France, the principal battleground, was ravaged, and the British Empire had suffered a blow from which it never recovered.

How did this happen? What is it about the situation in July and August 1914 that made it so difficult for experienced government leaders to cope with it?

One factor was that suddenly, seemingly paramount interests were at stake. Moscow's credibility as protector of Serbia, its ally, and hence by implication its credibility toward all its allies, came into question. Berlin's credibility toward an ally was at stake too. Germany also ran the risk of being caught unprepared by a Russian attack.

Another critical problem was that both the tsar and Kaiser Wilhelm felt intense time pressure. They were dealing with threats and mobilizations that demanded immediate response. To compound these difficulties, the decision makers had little clear knowledge of the intentions of others. They had incomplete knowledge even about key events as they were taking place. No one could be certain about how others would respond to their decisions.

Finally, when they looked at the range of usable choices apparently before them, the options seemed few and extreme. In the end, they seemed to have seen only two: capitulation or war.

Each of the major governments involved faced its own particular threats and had its own particular choices to make. But behind these particulars lay four factors that were common to each one, and dangerous for everyone: high stakes, short time, great uncertainties, and few apparent options.

These four factors are present to varying degrees in all great international crises; the more acute the crisis, the more pervasive their impact. In combination, they have effects that even experienced government leaders often do not foresee and hence do not forestall. Together, they create a "warp" in human decision making that can cause seemingly rational decision making to yield an irrational outcome.

High Stakes

High stakes, most notably the risk of all-out war, are the most obvious element in a crisis. Without high stakes, decision makers may see themselves as putting out sparks but not as confronting a real crisis.

In a crisis, either the actual size of the stakes may rise or simply the chances of imminent loss, or both. With the arrival of tanks during the Checkpoint Charlie confrontation in Berlin in 1961, the stakes rose dramatically from an important point of diplomatic procedure to include a significant risk of combat between American and Soviet troops. At the same time, in the minds of Western leaders, the risk of losing West Berlin suddenly increased.

Often one side will deliberately raise the stakes, hoping thereby to compel the other side to back down. This is what Gamal Abdel Nasser did, for instance, in 1967. In response to reports that Israel was about to attack Syria, the Egyptian leader closed the Gulf of Aqaba to Israel. He thought that Israel would accept a political setback rather than start a war. He was wrong. Israel launched pre-emptive air and tank strikes and won the war in six days.

Little Time

In the spring of 1958, Premier Nikita Khrushchev threatened to take unilateral action in Berlin unless the issues about its future were resolved by the end of the year. As the summer became fall, the sense of crisis mounted in the West.

As the deadline drew near, however, the Soviets backed off and signaled that nothing drastic would happen when it passed. There is a story, possibly apocryphal, that Khrushchev, asked when the Soviets would act, replied, "Well, if not this December, then some December."

This imposition and then removal of a deadline demonstrates one of the central elements in what makes a crisis a crisis: the pressure of time. However grave the issues, conflict does not become crisis as long as plenty of time is available. Having enough time to decide may make the difference between peace and war. George Ball, one of Kennedy's senior advisers during the Cuban missile crisis, reports that when he and other former advisers met again many years later, "much to our own surprise, we reached the unanimous conclusion that, had we determined our course of action within the first forty-eight hours after the missiles were discovered, we would almost certainly have made the wrong decision, responding to the missiles in such a way as to require a forceful Soviet response and thus setting in train a series of reactions and counter-reactions with horrendous consequences."

Sometimes, of course, decision makers will deliberately reduce the time available for decision as a way of escalating a crisis. The classic method is the ultimatum, with its tight deadline.

High Uncertainty

One aspect of crises leaders often emphasize is the great uncertainties they faced. They recall feeling as if they were groping in a fog.

This uncertainty may take at least three different forms. The simplest is a lack of critical *information* about what is going on. Are the opponent's forces mobilized? Where are they deployed? Are they moving? What exactly is occurring? The facts available are nearly always incomplete.

Usually decision makers are also uncertain about the other

side's *intentions.* Do they have one limited objective in mind, whose attainment might be tolerable? Or do they have bigger ambitions, and if so, how much bigger?

Closely related is great uncertainty about the likely *escalation sequence.* How will they respond to our action? What will we do then? And how will they react to that? It is often difficult to see more than one or two steps down the road.

In the 1973 Mideast war all three kinds of uncertainty were present. On October 22, for instance, American intelligence spotted radiation from nuclear materials being shipped through the Bosporus in Soviet ships. Were these nuclear weapons? Or merely fuel rods being shipped to some reactor, or perhaps just nuclear waste products?

If they were nuclear weapons, what did it mean? Did Leonid Brezhnev intend to make a drastic threat shortly? Or even, conceivably, *use* nuclear weapons in the Middle East? Or was he merely expecting that the West, spotting the radiation, would quickly become very cautious?

If a drastic threat was made, what events would follow? What if the Israelis rejected the Soviet demand? What if the Soviets intervened militarily? Could it conceivably escalate to nuclear weapons? Each of these "ifs" was highly unlikely, but with such immensely high stakes, even a small uncertainty remained troubling.

The uncertainty intrinsic in every crisis is sometimes increased unnecessarily, because one party fails to communicate its intentions and interests. For instance, the deception the Soviets practiced before and during the Cuban missile crisis left American leaders highly uncertain about the real Soviet intentions. Moscow communicated little about the interests it was trying to further by placing missiles in Cuba, leaving the Americans to guess.

Sometimes serious warnings are given but go unheeded. In their memoirs, President Nixon and Secretary of State Henry Kissinger each report having received strongly worded warnings from Brezhnev in June 1973 that the Arabs would soon launch a war unless diplomatic efforts progressed on securing Israeli withdrawal from territories occupied in 1967. Interpreting this as just the usual Soviet bluster, however, the American leaders dismissed the warnings.

Few Options

In a crisis, decision makers typically see themselves as having few usable options, with those available often lying at the extremes. Options in a crisis are "sliced thick" compared to normal times, when many more finely sliced options are available or can be developed. During the first forty-eight hours of the Cuban missile crisis, American decision makers in the White House discussed seriously only two options: taking no military action while resorting to diplomacy, or carrying out an air strike on Cuba that might have triggered a perilous escalation. The option of the quarantine was developed only later.

The Cuban missile crisis was intense from the outset. In crises that have developed gradually, policymakers usually see their options narrowing as the escalation intensifies. Finally, the choices seem to be reduced to two: go to war or back down. This is what happened in World War I.

Sometimes leaders fail to generate a larger range of options, in part because of the tendency in crisis decision making to exclude dissenting voices. Shortly after Kennedy became president, the CIA presented a plan to him for a secret operation to use Cuban émigrés to invade Cuba and overthrow Fidel Castro. Kennedy neither requested nor was offered any credible alternatives. Thus, he faced the choice of executing a risky plan or incurring heavy bureaucratic and political costs by not acting at all. By executing the plan, he fell into the Bay of Pigs fiasco.

Decision makers may also deliberately foreclose options

that could defuse a crisis. This strategy, known as a "commitment strategy," resembles the game of chicken, graphically illustrated by Thomas Schelling's anecdote of two dynamite trucks barreling toward each other on a single-lane road. The question is, which truck will go off the road to avoid a collision? They come closer and closer until one driver, in full view of the other, pulls off his steering wheel and throws it out the window. This leaves the other driver with the unpleasant choice between a crash and driving his truck off the road into a ditch.

International affairs rarely present choices this stark, but nations often do visibly decrease the options before them in order to demonstrate their commitment to one particular outcome. This strategy may strengthen one's bargaining position, but if both sides indulge in the commitment strategy during a crisis, they may narrow the options to only one: war.

The Decision Warp

The factors of high stakes, short time, high uncertainty, and few options combine to create among decision makers a pressure to act. They may not be consciously aware of all four factors during an actual crisis, but they certainly will be consciously aware of the result: a need "to *do* something." Calls from the public for "action" only intensify this need.

The pressure of the crisis is increased by the inevitable stress. Leaders become tense, anxious, and fatigued. The result is a kind of tunnel vision. Researchers have shown that people under stress tend to focus on the threats facing them and overlook feelers toward negotiation. As a result, decision makers often do not take steps that might be open to them to *reduce* the crisis factors. For instance, at a moment of intense confrontation, opening communications with the enemy hardly seems like an obvious option. Yet such a step might at least gain more time and reduce uncertainty. Instead, the four elements feeding on each other impel leaders to take some step they might well *not* take if they had more time, and if they used that time to create new options, reduce key uncertainties, and lower the stakes.

Unfortunately, the effect of this "decision warp" does not stop with one decision. In a crisis, the decision by one side to escalate inevitably has a powerful effect on leaders on the opposing side. It raises their stakes and reduces the time they feel they have available. It may increase their uncertainties and decrease their apparent options. In short, it worsens *their* decision warp. And that makes all the more likely a dangerous counterescalation, which then, in turn, worsens the warp on the first side. The spiral has begun. At some point a threshold is crossed and the crisis becomes a runaway, out of the control of the decision makers on either side.

Though it may be difficult to imagine exactly how incidents between nations might get out of control, a loose analogy can be found in everyday experience. It begins with "harmless" kidding around between two people with a problem. A serious exchange of words results, frustration increases, and then, without warning or conscious decisions to up the ante, some invisible threshold is crossed and violence, either emotional or physical, ensues. One thing led to another, even though neither of them intended it to get out of hand. But somehow it happened, and the consequences are as real as if it was all intentional from the start.

This is not altogether unlike the way a crisis may heat up between nations. High stakes, short time, high uncertainty, and few usable options combine to create a decision warp, which can distort the judgment of experienced, capable government leaders. This is the nub of what makes a crisis treacherous, what makes runaway escalation possible, and what may ignite a war no one originally intended.

How Did It Happen?

During the crisis of 1914, each of the most powerful leaders in the world tried to prevent or at least limit the war. But the spiral of escalation had escaped their control. We are fortunate that those who proceeded to make war did not have nuclear weapons at their disposal, just as we are fortunate that those who had the weapons found a way to avoid using them in the Cuban crisis of 1962. Crises and their aftermaths have lessons for the future. If we learn from them, we will be better prepared.

In 1914, just after the Austro-Hungarian crisis had turned into a general European war, Prince Bernhard von Bülow, former chancellor of Germany, is reputed to have asked his successor, "How did it happen?" "Ah, if only we knew," came the answer. The purpose of crisis control is to help ensure that von Bülow's question will never be asked in the nuclear age.

PART II

Creating a Crisis Control System

3

Beyond the Hotline

> The notion of a control system especially designed for critical periods admittedly sounds strange, but its strangeness is due to the fact that we still have not yet comprehended the revolutionary nature of our present world. The new [nuclear] technology can be mastered only by political innovations as dramatic as those in the field of science.
>
> Henry Kissinger, 1961

At ten o'clock in the morning on Wednesday, October 24, 1962, President Kennedy waited with his advisers for news of two Soviet ships and a Soviet submarine steadily approaching the American naval blockade at that very moment. If the vessels were to continue, they would have to be stopped and boarded, probably within half an hour. "I think these few minutes were the time of gravest concern for the President," Robert Kennedy later reflected. "Was the world on the brink of a holocaust? Was it our error? A mistake? Was there something further that should have been done? Or not done? [The President's] hand went up to his face and covered his mouth. He opened and closed his fist. His face seemed drawn, his eyes pained, almost gray. We stared at each other across the table. For a few fleeting seconds, it was almost as though no one else was there and he was no longer the President."

Was there indeed something further that should have been done — long in advance? What should the president have discussed beforehand with his Soviet counterpart? What procedures, institutions, and trained personnel should have been in place to give the president and the Soviet leaders the best chance to end the crisis on mutually acceptable terms, and indeed if possible to have prevented it in the first place?

Is a Crisis Control System Conceivable?

Since a crisis is almost by definition unpredictable, it may seem strange to think of a system for routinely preventing and dealing with one. Yet we live with such systems every day. A smoke detector monitors our hallways, a fire hydrant sits at the street corner, an ambulance waits at the local hospital, and a flight attendant points out the emergency exits on every flight. Intertwined with emergency procedures are preventive measures: A mechanic routinely checks the airplane, the doctor suggests a yearly physical, the bed mattress is made of nonflammable material. In each safety system, procedures, institutions, technology, and trained people all interact continuously to prevent and defuse a sudden life-threatening situation.

Even the notion that a system can stop a dangerous crisis between powerful and competing nations is not new. In the nineteenth century, the leaders of the Great Powers pioneered a crisis control system. Part of the Concert of Europe, it lasted for nearly a century.

For almost twenty years before 1814, all of Europe had been embroiled in the Napoleonic Wars. When the carnage finally ended, the shocked leaders of Europe determined, as one historian puts it, that "only collective action designed to forestall cataclysmic war would guarantee future survival.

The chief architects of the new order therefore began to speak explicitly of the need for a 'system' based upon what was 'best for the general interest.' "

For a hundred years thereafter, Europe enjoyed "an epoch of unprecedented peace." Smaller wars did break out, of course, but there was no general European war. The system was far from perfect, yet it offers certain lessons for today.

Despite their ancient feuds, the statesmen of Europe worked together, regulated their competition, and established a kind of collective security. Their chief tool was consultation with one another. Whenever a threat to the peace emerged, representatives of the Great Powers would come together. They sought to make any needed changes in the political map through negotiation. When the Belgians revolted in 1830, the statesmen of Europe assembled to prevent a dangerous scramble by the Great Powers to seize the territory. In the end, they agreed to make Belgium independent and neutral. In 1867 they moved to protect Luxembourg, and in 1878 they dealt with explosive Balkan conflicts.

It was understood that no nation would take military action while an international conference met to cope with a crisis. So the very calling of a conference kept the stakes from rising and bought precious time to negotiate. In turn, the negotiations helped reduce each nation's uncertainty and create new options for a diplomatic solution. Crises were thus defused.

Gradually, however, the fear of a cataclysmic war faded and statesmen began to take the system for granted. Tragically, the Concert of Europe fell into disuse at the very time it was most needed — during the tense years leading up to World War I. When Prince von Bülow's successor exclaimed in 1914, "Ah, if only we knew," he spoke of a world in which crisis control had been largely abandoned.

Today, the world is very different. The easy paternalism of great powers is no longer readily accepted. Mobilization for war takes not days and months but hours and minutes. All the same, the Concert of Europe remains a vivid reminder that the leaders of opposing nations can invent a system to control crises and prevent a cataclysm none of them wants.

Crisis Control Enters the Nuclear Age

American and Soviet leaders began to reinvent bits and pieces of crisis control during the cold war crises of the 1950s, but it was the Cuban missile crisis, above all, that dramatized the need for a "system" to prevent runaway escalation. "There is no longer any such thing as strategy, only crisis management," Robert McNamara announced to a congressional committee in the wake of the confrontation.

Time after time during those tense days, President Kennedy and Premier Khrushchev demonstrated their determination to keep the crisis under control. Take, for instance, Kennedy's insistence that he be given more options than air strikes or a mere diplomatic protest. Even after the quarantine was devised and decided upon, Kennedy continued to move cautiously, always sensitive to how Khrushchev would react. When the Soviet ships approached the blockade, he sent a message on an open channel accessible to the Soviets, ordering the navy to delay boarding until the last possible moment. He furthermore allowed the first ship, the Soviet oil tanker *Bucharest,* to pass unchallenged through the blockade and instead carefully chose as the first ship to be stopped the *Marucla,* an American-built Panamanian-owned ship operating under a Soviet charter.

In all these actions, he sought to give Khrushchev time to reflect and reconsider. "What guided all his deliberations," Robert Kennedy noted later, "was an effort . . . not to have [the Soviets] feel they would have to escalate their response because their national security or national interests so com-

The Cuban Missile Crisis. October 1962: A session of the Executive Committee. President Kennedy is at right, leaning over the table. To his left are Dean Rusk and Robert McNamara. Vice-President Johnson is at the center and Robert Kennedy is standing at the left. (Courtesy of the John F. Kennedy Library)

mitted them." He added, "We were not going to misjudge, or miscalculate, or challenge the other side needlessly, or precipitously push our adversaries into a course of action that was not intended or anticipated."

Khrushchev, too, showed considerable restraint once the crisis began. For instance, at the last minute the Soviet ships carrying missiles stopped and turned around rather than challenge the blockade. In a vivid letter Khrushchev wrote to Kennedy at the height of the crisis, he expressed his concern about how easily provocative steps could send the crisis spiraling out of control:

> If you have not lost your self-control and sensibly conceive what this might lead to, then, Mr. President, we and you ought not to pull on the ends of the rope in which you have tied the knot of war, because the more the two of us pull, the tighter the knot will be tied. And a moment may come when the knot will be tied so tight that not even he who tied it will . . . have the strength to untie it, and then it will be necessary to cut that knot, and what that could mean is not for me to explain to you because you yourself understand perfectly of what terrible forces our countries dispose.

Both Kennedy and Khrushchev were observing a key principle for controlling crises: Don't provoke the other side unnecessarily. Provocative actions raise the stakes and reduce the time available. An American air strike would have killed Russians, thereby raising the stakes for the Kremlin, and it would have demanded an almost immediate response. Khrushchev might well have retaliated, in Berlin or elsewhere. In opting for the quarantine, Kennedy was able to minimize the provocation.

A second important principle, also observed by Kennedy and Khrushchev, is to maximize mutual consultation. They exchanged messages by personal letters and through direct emissaries. On their behalf, Anatoly Dobrynin, the Soviet ambassador, and Robert Kennedy met several times to seek a solution. In 1962 the letters and personal meetings lowered both sides' uncertainties and made it possible for the president and the premier to find options they could agree on.

Minimizing provocation helps keep the stakes from rising and buys time for both sides to think and talk. Maximizing consultation helps reduce dangerous uncertainty and create options acceptable to each side. In this fashion, all four critical factors of a crisis can be mitigated.

If the Cuban missile crisis had led to war, historians would have had little difficulty explaining why. Deep-seated geopolitical and ideological conflicts, a spiraling arms race, and the heightened tension of the cold war made a clash seem all but inevitable, yet the crisis did not turn into a war. Leaders on each side preserved the peace through successful crisis control.

Still, the confrontation came far too close to war for comfort or complacency. Far better than defusing a full-blown crisis, therefore, is catching it early on, before it escalates to superpower confrontation. Preventing or putting out any sparks that could conceivably ignite a nuclear crisis is another essential element of crisis control. When in May 1967 Lyndon Johnson tried to stave off war between Israel and Egypt, or when in 1983 Moscow warned Washington to limit its air attacks to Lebanon in order not to involve the Soviet advisers manning the air defenses of Syria, they were engaging in crisis control. It is not an activity that goes on only during an acute U.S.-Soviet crisis. It is an ongoing effort, most effective when no one hears about it because it has headed off a crisis before one occurred.

Crisis Control Since 1962: Steps Toward a System

During the Cuban missile crisis, Kennedy and Khrushchev had to improvise a system to minimize provocation and maximize communication. Time seemed short. But in a new crisis today, it might be even shorter. The press of time, as in a fire or medical crisis, requires that a system be set up in advance.

Consider the problem of communication. During the 1962 crisis, normal diplomatic channels proved too slow and cumbersome. Kennedy and Khrushchev found they had to improvise direct communication. At one point, the chargé d'affaires at the Soviet embassy in Washington telephoned an ABC News correspondent to deliver a message. Midnight meetings in Washington restaurants became a way for the two sides to talk. In order to tell Kennedy in time that he was withdrawing the missiles, Khrushchev had to broadcast the message on the radio.

Both sides realized this was extremely inadequate. The crisis proved how important it was for the heads of state to communicate with each other secretly, directly, and quickly. Shortly thereafter, Washington and Moscow became linked by the Hotline.

Contrary to popular belief, the Hotline is not a red telephone sitting on the president's desk. It is a Teletype located in the Pentagon with an extension to the White House. Voice contact, officials feared, would create too high a risk of misunderstanding through immediate translation and hasty response. A printed message allows more time to reflect and to consult advisers before responding.

Since 1963, Washington and Moscow have agreed on further measures to reduce the likelihood of provocative behavior, improve crisis communication, and prevent sparks from igniting a crisis in the first place. Following are the major steps in the chronology of crisis control:

- 1971. The Hotline is made more reliable. Two satellite links are added; the sea and land link is kept as a back-up.
- 1971. The United States and the USSR sign the so-called Accidents Agreement. It commits each side to notifying the other at once in the event of an accidental unauthorized occurrence that could lead to a threatening detonation; to give notice of any missile test firings in the direction of the other's homeland; "to act in such a way as to reduce the possibility" of actions being misinterpreted should a nuclear incident occur; and to maintain and im-

prove internal arrangements intended to prevent unauthorized or accidental nuclear war.

- 1972. The Incidents at Sea Agreement creates navigation rules for naval vessels and procedures for coping with accidental collisions and near-misses.
- 1972. The Basic Principles Agreement attempts to create a mutual understanding about the ground rules for Soviet-American involvement in the Third World.
- 1973. The Prevention of Nuclear War Agreement requires consultation between Washington and Moscow in any situation carrying a higher than normal risk of nuclear war.
- 1975. An agreement on confidence-building measures in Europe requires prior notification of major military maneuvers in Europe and provides for the exchange of observers at these maneuvers.
- 1984. The Hotline is improved again, gaining the capability to transmit whole pages of text, photographs, and graphics.

These agreements are the first important steps toward creating a full-fledged crisis control system for the nuclear age. Such a system would consist of basic understandings and of procedures and institutions for implementing them.

The understandings largely exist already. The Accidents Agreement of 1971 and the Prevention of Nuclear War Agreement of 1973 commit both superpowers to exert every effort to avert the outbreak of nuclear war through increasing consultation in time of danger, avoiding provocation, and preventing incidents that could spark a crisis.

Both agreements, however, have been half forgotten. Their general phrases were seen by many as empty rhetoric, and the specific measures were understood as applying only to a narrow spectrum of nuclear dangers, and then only at the last moment. But the dramatically increased concern on both sides about nuclear war could help breathe new life and power into the principles already negotiated. These principles could become the underpinnings of a crisis control system that would not only swing into action at the last possible moment but function at all times to help prevent "the last moment" from ever arriving. Runaway escalation can and should be stopped well before it starts.

This system can go beyond the Hotline to include continuous face-to-face interaction between specially trained diplomats and military officers at a crisis control center. It can go beyond the Incidents at Sea Agreement to encompass analogous safety procedures to prevent dangerous incidents of all types. It can add to the urgent consultations required by the Prevention of Nuclear War Agreement a set of regular crisis control consultations at the ministerial level. It would include preparing the president and his senior advisers more extensively. And it would mean further development of a fallback strategy for dealing with an adversary in crisis who at first may be more interested in unilateral gain than in avoiding steps that might lead to nuclear war. These proposals appear in the chapters that follow.

A Word of Caution

First, however, a word of caution is in order. A crisis control system is not without pitfalls and risks. Crisis control contains a basic paradox. The very information that leaders should have during a crisis in order to control and end it is often the same information that, if available before the crisis, might lead to overconfidence. Having a crisis control system could conceivably cause leaders to relax in times of crisis or even to take risks they would not take without the system. However, just as people did not turn their backs on the invention of smoke detectors for fear everyone would grow careless with matches, so it would not be wise for this reason alone to pass up creating a new generation of crisis control measures.

A more concrete danger of many such measures lies in their vulnerability to misuse. Unless adequate safeguards are adopted, a joint center could be used for gathering intelligence or for sending false information at a critical time. Moreover, unless allies and friends are carefully consulted, a crisis control system could be misinterpreted as collusion by the superpowers to control the world.

Finally, some fear that the creation of a crisis control system could breed a false confidence that the nuclear danger has been disposed of and that efforts to reduce weapons and improve relations could be relaxed. Ironically, crisis control, far from being a rival approach, is a twin. Just as emergency care and regular monitoring can give a heart disease patient the time to implement a long-term prevention program of diet and exercise, so effective crisis control can help provide the time needed for genuine and significant arms reductions and for developing a better working relationship between the United States and the USSR. There is no room for complacency in working toward limiting weapons and relaxing tensions, nor is there any in working toward preventing the runaway escalation of a crisis.

Each of the measures described in the chapters that follow is a small practical step to reduce the risk of nuclear war. Taken together, they help constitute a crisis control system. They are not intended to be comprehensive, however. In a sense, such a system will never be complete but will always evolve in response to newly appreciated dangers. As with a fire prevention system, the construction of a crisis control system is a continuing process.

Again, just as the prevention of a citywide fire is not the only objective of a fire prevention system, so the prevention of nuclear war is not the only goal of crisis control. Both kinds of systems serve to eliminate many lesser but still highly significant dangers. Indeed, the successful prevention of a single conventional war, of a nuclear explosion, or of a tragic incident such as the 1983 downing of the Korean Air Lines plane would in itself justify the creation of a crisis control system.

Finally, the measures described here are presented not as a final blueprint but rather as ideas designed to stimulate discussion and to elicit criticism and improvements. They are intended to illustrate what could be done. Though each one has its own specific merits (and risks), what matters most is the overall approach for systematically controlling crises.

Like fires, crises are likely to recur. With a modern fire control system, however, individual fires may start again and again, but the whole city will not burn.

4

A Joint Crisis Control Center

A little fire is quickly trodden out,
Which, being suffered, rivers cannot quench.

William Shakespeare
Henry IV, Part III, Act 4, Scene 8

Imagine that war breaks out between Israel and Syria. As they did in 1967, Israeli tanks gather on the Golan Heights, as if preparing for an attack on Damascus. Grimly determined to deter Israel, Moscow issues a verbal threat as it did in 1967 but goes further by placing part of its military forces on a higher state of alert. The next day, Washington counters with a worldwide alert of conventional and nuclear forces of the kind it called in 1973. In doing so, each side removes certain safeguards against inadvertent use of nuclear weapons.

That midnight the news flashes into Washington that San Francisco has just been destroyed in a nuclear explosion. Quickly, the North American Air Defense Command

(NORAD), located under a mountain in Colorado, determines that no other nuclear detonations have occurred and that no missiles seem to be on the way.

The president and his advisers face an extraordinary uncertainty. What has destroyed San Francisco? Is this event connected with the Middle East war? Is it the act of a terrorist group that has acquired a nuclear weapon? Is it some terrible accident, involving an American weapon? Or was it the Russians?

The Hotline starts printing out a message from Moscow. The general secretary disavows any responsibility and offers his sympathies. He offers to make available any proof he can that this was not a Soviet attack and that no attack is contemplated. He says he has directed the Soviet staff at the crisis control center to cooperate in every way with the Americans in providing proof and in helping to identify the true cause.

Many in Washington are suspicious. Soviet submarines with both cruise and ballistic missiles are known to be not far out in the Pacific. U.S. radar data that night are incomplete and no one can be positive that no missile arrived from the west. No messages have been received from any terrorists. The United States has been dealt a horrible blow. Why shouldn't it be the Soviets? The Pentagon insists on putting U.S. nuclear forces on an even higher degree of alert.

The center swings into action. Within an hour, a teleconference begins among the American and Soviet staff officers in Moscow and Washington. The atmosphere is tense, but officers on both sides of the table in both capitals know each other well. They have discussed contingencies like this one often. They have experience in dealing with each other in this way, talking face to face, or viewing each other on bigger-than-life television screens that cover nearly an entire wall in the main conference room at each location. The Americans in Washington and the Soviets in Moscow have many lines

U.S.-Soviet Crisis Control Center. An artist's rendering of the joint center, where trained staff from each nation would monitor crises around the clock, relaying vital information in person, as well as by telephone, computer, and teleconferencing. In time of crisis, the center would function somewhat like the emergency room of a hospital, providing a place and resources to enable the principals to deal with a critical situation as effectively and expeditiously as possible. (Drawing by Michael Eagle)

of communication into their own governments, through which questions and information now pour. The meeting goes on for hours.

In their own self-interest, the Soviets provide demonstrative reassurances and important information. The Soviet subs currently in the eastern Pacific are ordered to the surface, for U.S. aerial verification of their location and to show they do not seek to hide from American retaliation. When the U.S. Navy cannot quickly find one of the seven, the center's staff officers, working together, discover a minor error in the location data that had been provided. The final sub is found. The United States tracks them all but takes no action.

At the center, the Soviets provide extensive data from their radar ground stations, giving complete tracks (insofar as they have them) of all flying objects in the eastern Pacific and polar regions for the last few hours. The Soviets also provide radar and infrared data from their satellites (two of which passed over the eastern Pacific in the hours preceding the explosion) about the location and course of surface ships, including one ship of Middle Eastern registry about which relatively little is known. All this information appears on a huge electronic map in the center.

The Americans receive all this data with some skepticism, which redoubles when they discover that it does not entirely match similar American data about air and sea traffic. But the center's staff, working jointly on the discrepancies, discovers gradually that they result from differences in Soviet and American technology and data-gathering techniques, and in several instances from human or computer error in processing and transmission.

Some of the Soviet and American officers at the center begin to focus on a problem they had recently been discussing: Within the last six weeks they had considered the possibility that a U.S. nuclear weapon, now missing, may have been stolen; and they had discussed some evidence suggesting that it could have fallen into the hands of one of several fanatical Middle Eastern groups.

While all this is occurring, another small group of center staff officers is focusing on the dangerous interaction that has been going on between the two sides' warning systems and nuclear forces. The new U.S. strategic alert, instantly observed by Soviet satellites, has caused all sorts of actions to be taken in the USSR as a matter of standard procedure. Radar and communications systems have been turned on, air and missile crews assembled, airborne and underground command centers activated, and so forth. These actions have, in turn, been observed by the U.S. warning system, and additional actions taken, again as standard procedure, to increase further the U.S. ability to gather information.

The center staff, like their superiors in Washington and Moscow, are concerned that these actions back and forth could continue to "ratchet upward," as each side responds to the other side's responses. The American officers explain to their Soviet colleagues the way various American procedures are being triggered by Soviet actions; and the Soviet officers do the same. Working with others in various command centers in the United States and the USSR, the center officers informally work out a "plateau" at which this process can be stopped. No further alerting actions will be taken beyond that plateau without a top-level decision in Washington or Moscow.

Four and a half hours after the center's teleconference began, the president and his advisers decide to lower the level of the American strategic alert by one notch. Nine hours thereafter, they are sufficiently convinced by the Soviet data, and by Soviet behavior now, that they call off the alert and return U.S. nuclear forces to their normal posture. An immense intelligence effort is now launched. Washington seeks assistance from more than a dozen friends and allies to ascertain whether the destruction of San Francisco was indeed an act of terrible retaliation, by a terrorist group, against U.S. policies in the Middle East. It is a major international crisis, but it is no longer an acute U.S.-Soviet crisis, and it does not pose a significant risk of nuclear war between the superpowers.

Is this scenario likely? No. Is it possible? Unfortunately, yes. So are many other scenarios for unintended U.S.-Soviet nuclear confrontation.

The Center Proposal

The most tangible step to take beyond the Hotline toward a crisis control system is a center, jointly staffed around the clock by the United States and the Soviet Union. Military and diplomatic officers at this center would work together to forestall crises and would help to end quickly and safely any that do occur.

Proposals for such a crisis control center have been introduced during the past few years in the United States Senate. The best known bore the sponsorship of the late Senator Henry Jackson (D–Washington) and Senators Sam Nunn (D–Georgia) and John Warner (R–Virginia). It was a later version of this plan that was passed by the Senate in June 1984. Earlier that year, the Reagan administration took an initial step toward a center by proposing to the Soviets the establishment of a "Joint Military Communications Link," a working hotline between the military headquarters on each side for more regular exchange of time-sensitive military information.

Early versions of the center idea pictured a single center at a neutral location such as Vienna or Helsinki. But as many have pointed out, that kind of center would be too far from the hubs of decision making and therefore, in time of crisis, too difficult to use.

The center might best begin with twin locations — in

Washington and Moscow — electronically linked by telephone, computer, facsimile transmission, and teleconferencing. In Washington there might be eight American staff officers and four Soviets; in Moscow the numbers would be reversed. Staff would rotate between the two sites. The American officers in Washington and the Soviet officers in Moscow would also meet frequently with officials and working groups in various departments of their own governments.

The Hotline is simply not enough. It is an extremely valuable instrument, but it has significant limitations. The essential communications between the U.S. and Soviet sides in the San Francisco scenario probably could not have been adequately conducted by the Hotline. That kind of resolution requires many people, complex discussions, and fast work. It benefits from face-to-face conversations by trained specialists who have developed a working relationship before the crisis occurs.

Consider a loose analogy: If you had to work out a complex, high-stakes deal with a company on the other side of the country in an extremely short time, would you try to do it by sending telegrams back and forth? Nothing really substitutes for talking face to face, where the personalities, the emotions, the dynamics, and the body language around the words can all be appropriately taken into account. What is more, communication will be more productive if the people on both sides already know each other, have worked together, and have prepared themselves individually and jointly for just such circumstances. Consider how much easier it is to deal with someone in a time of difficulty when you have collaborated in the past.

Many communications, moreover, would be inappropriate for the Hotline, not important enough to be transmitted from head of state to head of state. It has typically been used for carrying short messages during intense crises. The Hotline is not designed for working-level discussions that need to take place both before and after the major decisions have been made.

In time of crisis, the center would be like the emergency room of a hospital, providing a place and resources to enable the principals to deal with the problem as effectively and expeditiously as possible. The center would also have a preventive role, operating like a well-baby clinic, providing regular checkups, monitoring potential problems, and ensuring that any early warning signs do not go unaddressed.

The Center in a Crisis

The center and its personnel in Washington and Moscow could perform five broad tasks in a crisis.

Exchanging, clarifying, and authenticating complex information. Back-and-forth communication to eliminate dangerous misunderstandings is the essence of what a center would do. As the San Francisco scenario illustrates, the officers could jointly examine and discuss relevant data. Since computer print-outs, photographs, and diagrams can easily be misinterpreted, American and Soviet specialists need to assess them jointly. And since the atmosphere is naturally one of distrust, the opportunity to question and challenge the authenticity of the other side's information and interpretation is critical.

Carrying out emergency safety procedures. In the San Francisco scenario, the center officers carry out a procedure carefully worked out beforehand by both sides for the precise contingency of a detonation of mysterious origin. This is but one of many emergencies to which the center would respond with special procedures created ahead of time.

Consider, for instance, what might have happened if the center had existed in September 1983, when Korean Air

Lines flight 007 strayed into Soviet airspace. The Soviet air defense command might have immediately queried the American experts at the Moscow crisis control center about the nature and mission of the Korean airliner as it intruded. "An unidentified plane has violated our airspace. We will be forced to shoot it down if it continues on its present course." Working rapidly through the use of information-retrieval systems in America, and perhaps with the assistance of Japanese radar as well, the American experts in Moscow might have succeeded in identifying the plane as a KAL civilian 747. They could then have worked together with their Soviet counterparts to make radio contact with the plane in order to direct it immediately out of Soviet territory or to a safe landing spot for Soviet inspection.

Technical problem solving. Perhaps the most dangerous crises are those least expected. When every minute may count, a trained binational staff used to working with each other and ready on an instant's notice to engage in intensive ad hoc problem solving could make a critical difference. The staff could not make political decisions, but once the leaders decided, they could work out the technical details of implementation.

In certain cases, they might even be called upon to explore creative options, especially if it was understood from the outset that they did *not* have the authority to negotiate for their governments. During the SALT I negotiations, admittedly a different context, both governments found it useful to have a couple of junior officials on each side meet regularly to explore options without commitment. Known informally as "the wizards," these officials were knowledgeable and bilingual, but lower level, and therefore easy to disavow.

What could the center do if, for instance, another war broke out between India and Pakistan? This time both sides might have nuclear weapons. As an ally of Pakistan, the United States might send warships to the area, as it did during the India-Pakistan war of 1971. As India's friend, the Soviet Union would likely respond by sending its navy. With neither superpower fully intending it, a hazardous situation of great potential danger could rapidly develop: American and Soviet ships close to each other and on opposite sides of a conflict that could quickly turn nuclear. As they jockeyed for superior position, a series of isolated collisions could escalate into a full-fledged naval battle.

Before this came even close to happening, high-level American and Soviet officials would try, as they have in the past, to work out some general rules of nonengagement, such as a fixed distance each side's ships would keep from the other's. If a crisis control center existed, its staff could be called upon for working-level discussions of technical details and procedures for verifying mutual compliance.

Experts on call. In focusing on what role the institution could play, it is vital not to overlook the individuals involved, for they might prove to be the chief resource in a crisis. When in tense times the drawbridge is raised and only a tiny number of leaders are meeting to decide, some of the center's specialists might be tapped for their expertise even if the institution itself is not formally used in that particular crisis. From studying past crises and current leadership styles, they would be uniquely knowledgeable about the ways their own nation and the other superpower make decisions in time of crisis. They would thus serve as a human repository of the accumulated wisdom from past crises and of expertise for handling future ones.

If another India-Pakistan war broke out, the center staff would already have studied American and Soviet actions in the 1971 war, including various ways a new war in the area might escalate. Americans familiar with Soviet crisis decision making might be asked to help interpret Soviet actions or to design American actions so that they convey the message intended. The Soviet staff might be asked to play a similar role in Moscow.

Building public confidence. Consider the San Francisco scenario once more. If a nuclear bomb did explode, there would be shock and tremendous confusion, with the potential for panic all over the world. Is this the beginning of a war? Public hysteria could make it difficult for each side's leaders, particularly those in the United States, to go about resolving this new crisis calmly and effectively.

In such a moment it would be extremely useful to have reassuring symbols that demonstrate to the public that each superpower is cooperating with the other to try to defuse the crisis. The center would be even more visible than the Hotline has become. The public knowledge that Americans and Soviets were working intensively side by side at the center to avoid a war might allay anxiety and give the leaders of the United States and the USSR some time and room to communicate and deliberate.

For Normal Times: Work Toward Preventing War

What would the center do in normal times? Would there be challenging enough work to engage the kind of people able to handle a crisis? Actually, the responsibilities between crises would be, in some respects, more difficult and more important than those when the tension level was at its highest. In a time of near-war, heads of state and senior diplomats would be heavily involved and the center would serve a crucial, but primarily staff, function. In normal times, in addition to training and preparation for carrying out emergency procedures, the center's staff would work hard to prevent crises from taking place. Here are five specific functions that the center could be expected to perform during periods of calm:

Developing technical procedures. How can one side prove to the other that a launch was really an accident or was unauthorized? Or if Soviet and American naval units find themselves drawn into a local battle, how can a cease-fire be reached quickly? The crisis might be more quickly resolved if the center staff had analyzed these possibilities ahead of time and had created procedures for coping with them. Center staff could engage in simulations to develop these procedures and to test them before using them in a crisis.

Identifying new dangers. Discussing past unintended incidents and analyzing hypothetical ones could reveal risks of runaway escalation that the two sides had not talked about together, nor perhaps even fully appreciated themselves.

For instance, the center would be an ideal setting for coping with a dangerous coincidence of accidents and misinterpretations in a time of acute tension, such as the incredible coincidence described earlier that took place during the Suez crisis in November 1956. Such coincidences are hard to anticipate; a device such as the center is needed to deal with them as they occur. A question-and-answer dialogue by teleconference could clarify what was actually occurring. And the center staff would have practiced bringing together many kinds of relevant information and coping with simulated coincidences.

Exchanging information about global nuclear dangers. Building on their tradition of cooperation in trying to control nuclear proliferation, the United States and the Soviet Union could exchange information about potential sources of nuclear terrorism, and perhaps information about emerging risks of nuclear war in the Third World. Actually, in the talks on enhancing the Hotline, the U.S. government proposed just such an exchange to the Soviets, who reportedly listened with great interest. Conceivably, the center staff could go so far as to identify actions the two superpowers could take together to forestall nuclear terrorism or strengthen nonproliferation.

Questioning military movements and other threatening actions. The center could be as effective in normal times as during crises, clarifying the meaning of suspicious events. For instance, suppose the Soviet Union sends a task force of naval vessels in the direction of India at the same time as a major political upset there? Have the natural concerns of other nations about this coincidence been considered? In recent years the United States, the Soviet Union, and the nations of Europe have begun agreeing to confidence-building measures, committing themselves to informing one another in advance of planned military movements. Being able to discuss what the movements mean is a logical next step.

Staffing cabinet-level talks on crisis control. The center would be able to provide staff support, briefings, and a logical site for meetings on crisis control between cabinet-level officers from each side. Such close work during normal times would make it more likely that high-level decision makers would avail themselves of the center's expertise should a crisis erupt.

Starting the Center

Is it realistic and reasonable to envision a productive degree of U.S.-Soviet cooperation at the center? There is a positive precedent. Called the Standing Consultative Commission (SCC), it was established in 1972 as a by-product of the SALT

I Treaty. The SCC consists of a small American team of approximately fifteen working-level officers, a commissioner who is a diplomat, a deputy commissioner who is a military official, and a similar Soviet team. They hold two regularly scheduled sessions a year. Commissioners have the authority to call a special session whenever circumstances warrant.

Although it is unheralded, by the accounts of most observers the SCC has worked well, exceeding initial expectations. The original agreement specified that the two sides would provide, on a voluntary basis, information that either considered necessary for compliance with the SALT I Treaty. Most Americans were skeptical about whether the Soviets would provide any information on a voluntary basis, but they were surprised. According to Ambassador Sydney Graybeal, U.S. commissioner to the SCC from 1973 to 1976, "The Soviets have gone beyond what was necessary to remove U.S. concerns about some compliance issues." The success of the SCC stems in good part from the confidentiality of the proceedings. It takes both commissioners together to decide to make findings public. The SCC has a narrow, carefully defined mandate so that both sides concentrate on the specific problems at hand and not on wider political issues. Its work is conducted in a professional and businesslike spirit.

The crisis control center could start out resembling the SCC and build upon the successful precedent. Small at first, it could have a narrow and technical mandate, derived perhaps from the 1971 Accidents Agreement, to work on identifying, preventing, and controlling possible crises that would be wholly unintended, such as accidental or unauthorized launches, detonations of unknown origin, nuclear terrorism, and agent provocateur scenarios. These are the cases where the two sides share interests largely in common. Discussions could be informal and exploratory. Each government would understand that no suggestion could be taken as an official proposal.

As the center's personnel build up positive experience with this kind of joint work, and the respective governments see its usefulness, the scope can gradually expand to encompass problems where the two sides' interests are not entirely congruent, as in regional crises.

Wouldn't a Crisis Control Center Be Misused?

Particularly at the beginning, each side would naturally worry that the other might misuse the center. In the summer and early fall of 1962, the Soviet Union repeatedly denied any intention of installing offensive missiles in Cuba, at the very moment they were actually installing them. Wouldn't a center be used for such "disinformation"?

The concern is real. Perhaps the best protection is to be constantly aware of the danger and to follow the practice of the U.S. delegation to the SCC, which independently checks Soviet information for accuracy where possible. The risk of disinformation, however, is not significantly greater in a staffed center than it is in *any* communication medium, including the Hotline. Indeed, face-to-face communication may offer the opportunity to challenge statements as possible disinformation. In asking questions, one may derive a better sense of whether the truth is being told.

Would the center be used to gather intelligence about the other side? The Soviets express as much concern as the United States about this problem. For the SCC, the United States has developed a system of information filters that help protect against the danger of intelligence leaks. Though neither side can eliminate this risk altogether, the experience of the SCC suggests the possibility of minimizing it.

Yet another potential problem is that superpower collaboration at the center might appear threatening to both nations' allies, to China, and to the rest of the world. America's European allies, in particular, might fear that the existence of a crisis control center could encourage the old idea of a nuclear war limited to Europe. Moscow and Washington could reduce this risk considerably by emphasizing in advance, to all nations, the center's narrowly defined scope of cooperation and by consulting each side's allies about the center's design.

Finally, what about the problem of information overload during time of crisis? Adding channels of communication between the United States and the USSR may be seen as unnecessary and, worse, confusing because it increases the chance for misunderstanding. Adding another bureaucratic player might complicate the governmental decision-making process on each side, thereby reducing the head of state's flexibility. While these are not trivial problems, the center can be designed to minimize them. Indeed, on occasion, the center could actually enhance leaders' flexibility by offering additional options and critical information without binding either side.

All of these problems are real, but they lose much of their force against a carefully designed center that takes them into account, begins with a narrow mandate, and, as time passes, proves itself worthy to expand.

A crisis control center need not depend on trust or good will. Instead, it can depend on the self-interest that both nations share in avoiding an unintended war. As Senator Nunn once said about the center concept, "To work together in these areas does not require an assumption that the Soviet leaders are honest and trustworthy — only an assumption that they are sane."

As Senate Resolution 329 demonstrates, a joint crisis control center is an idea in the air these days. When the Hotline was first proposed, it, too, encountered objections as well as bureaucratic resistance. Some of the same arguments are now being raised against the center. Why talk with the enemy? Why expose yourself? Won't the other side use it to deceive? Isn't there a danger that the U.S. side might say something hasty or give away a secret?

Today, more than twenty years after the establishment of the Hotline, it is obvious that these objections are insignificant compared to its potential benefits. Everyone counts on the Hotline's being there should a crisis erupt. Twenty years after the center is established, people may look on it with the same feelings they have now about the Hotline: It is simple common sense. How did we ever do without it?

5

Emergency Safety Procedures

Peace is easily maintained;
Trouble is easily overcome before it starts . . .
Deal with it before it happens.
Set things in order before there is confusion.

Lao Tzu, *Tao Te Ching*
(circa 520 B.C.)

Korean Air Lines Flight 007: The "What Ifs"

On September 1, 1983, Korean Air Lines flight 007 strayed into Soviet airspace. Exactly how this happened is still not clear, but whatever the real story, the Soviet air force shot it down after about two hours. All 269 people aboard perished in the Sea of Japan. As the news became known, a wave of outrage spread throughout the world. The Soviets were denounced; some charged they had attacked the defenseless plane deliberately with full knowledge that it was a civilian aircraft. Others thought the sequence of Soviet actions suggested that decision makers in Moscow were not on top of events. Few things could have been more destructive to the Soviet campaign to stop the deployment of new missiles in

Europe, which the Kremlin leadership had been nurturing for years. Had the Soviet military, then, acted out of control?

On television and radio, people asked: How would the West respond? Would we retaliate? It was easy to recall the incident that set off World War I and wonder if the shooting down of flight 007 could become a similar spark for war.

There was anger and rhetoric from all sides. The Soviets suffered a serious public relations defeat, and many Western nations temporarily refused to allow Soviet planes to land at their airports. However, no serious escalation of the crisis took place.

In retrospect, apart from the human tragedy, the most worrisome questions are the "what ifs." What if the plane had been American — a Pan American flight, say, with 269 Americans aboard? And what if the attack had come during a time of severe international tension?

Whenever a sudden crisis erupts, many worry that it will be the time the match is set to the tinderbox of worldwide arms and animosities. What steps, then, can be taken now to avoid a nuclear Sarajevo in the future?

Again, fire safety procedures provide the best analogy. Catastrophic fires in Chicago in 1871, in Boston the following year, and in San Francisco in 1906 destroyed major portions of these cities and are still remembered today. That many of us are too young to have lived through such calamities bears testimony to the procedures people have created to help prevent fires and keep them from spreading.

Workers in factories now keep kerosene away from machinery that sparks, and flammable household fluids are so labeled. Fire exits are identified in movie theaters and nightclubs. Fire drills are part of every schoolchild's experience.

Preventive procedures help keep sparks from igniting a fire. Emergency procedures greatly reduce uncertainty about what to do if a fire does break out, uncertainty that might otherwise lead to panic. Similar procedures are needed to help prevent and control dangerous crises in the world. Agreeing on safety procedures beforehand could reduce dangerous uncertainty, enable rapid and accurate communication to take place, save precious time, and provide options for stepping back from the brink of war.

A Successful Model

A few safety procedures for crises already exist. The Incidents at Sea Agreement, mentioned before, had its origins in a series of actual close calls. As the Soviet navy became a global ocean-going force in the late 1960s, the number of encounters between American and Soviet naval vessels dramatically increased, triggering a dangerous competition. In order to test the other side and disrupt their operations, ships blocked, shouldered, and played chicken with each other. Admiral Elmo Zumwalt, later the highest-ranking American naval officer, recalls in his memoirs that when he was captain of an American destroyer, a Soviet frigate once tried to disrupt his ship's departure from a Norwegian port. The situation grew tense and a collision was only narrowly avoided.

As time went on, these incidents took on a life of their own. Captains retaliated and escalated; the intimidating behavior began to include the aiming of ship guns and missiles at an offending vessel. Planes even carried out mock dive bombings at the other side's ships.

On both sides, high-ranking military and civilian officials saw the danger of an incident erupting into a superpower crisis, especially in times of high tension. Quiet negotiation created a joint working group of naval officers who prepared an agreed-upon handbook of "rules of the road" and signals the two navies could use to communicate. Every ship in both navies received a copy. This not only gave ships at sea procedures by which they could avoid future incidents but also, more subtly, communicated throughout both navies that this kind of competitive behavior was not wanted.

Under the Incidents at Sea Agreement, high-ranking naval officers meet twice a year to review jointly any incidents that have occurred and to improve further, if necessary, the preventive procedures. In the event of a serious incident, either side can call a special meeting.

The agreement has led to a dramatic decrease in the number of near-misses and collisions. Although occasional close encounters still occur, both navies work to reduce them. It is honored not because of trust or good will, but simply because Washington and Moscow recognize a genuine common interest in ensuring that no hotheaded or careless action by two naval officers in some far-off corner of the globe triggers a dangerous crisis that neither side wants. They created a set of procedures, which each navy carries out through professional, low-level, confidential communication regardless of whether U.S.-Soviet relations at that point are good or bad. Indeed, it is precisely when relations are tense that these procedures are most valuable.

The principles of the Incidents at Sea Agreement can be extended to many kinds of sparks that could ignite an unintended war, where the dangers are specific and identifiable and the two countries share a common interest in coping with them. Following are examples of safety procedures for preventing or coping with close encounters between armed forces, regional conflicts, and freak detonations.

Safety Procedures for Close Encounters

Incidents in the Air Agreement. Hazardous and provocative incidents can occur in the air just as they can at sea. When a U.S. reconnaissance plane strayed into Soviet airspace at the height of the Cuban missile crisis, Khrushchev wrote to Kennedy:

> The question is, Mr. President, how should we regard this? What is this, a provocation? One of your planes violates our frontier during this anxious time we are both experiencing, when everything has been put into combat readiness. Is it not a fact that an intruding American plane could easily be taken for a nuclear bomber, which might push us to a fateful step?

The danger of an accidental air intrusion during an ongoing intense crisis makes agreed-upon procedures for coping with one particularly compelling. Such emergency safety procedures also could be valuable in normal times, for civilian as well as military planes. Had the Incidents at Sea Agreement been replicated in an Incidents in the Air Agreement, it is conceivable that the passengers on Korean Air Lines flight 007 might still be alive.

Agreement on Accidental Ground Intrusions. Occasionally, patrols lose their way and blunder across the border of NATO and Warsaw Pact countries. Or army helicopters, patrolling the ground near the frontiers, may stray over, as a U.S. Army helicopter did into Czechoslovakia in April 1984. So far, accidental ground intrusions have never generated an East-West crisis, and by themselves they are unlikely to. But suppose one occurred at a moment of intense crisis in Europe?

An Agreement on Accidental Ground Intrusions with procedures known to every relevant officer on each side might help. Like the Incidents at Sea Agreement, it could designate ranking officers from NATO and the Warsaw Pact nations who could communicate with one another directly to defuse an incident without its immediately escalating to an issue between Washington and Moscow.

The superpowers might extend this kind of understanding, perhaps informally, to other points where their forces come into close proximity. In 1983 and early 1984, for instance, American marines stationed in Beirut found themselves only about fifty miles from Soviet military personnel in Syria, at a time when fighting went on almost continuously among rival factions in Lebanon. U.S. Navy aircraft bombed positions between the marines and the Soviets, and at times the battleship *New Jersey* fired into the Lebanese melee. In that situation, American military commanders wisely took great care to keep their fire away from Soviet positions. But accidents can always occur. In some future tangle, where American and Soviet forces might be even closer and the regional fighting even more intense, the danger — and hence the need for understandings — would be even greater.

Agreements on ground incidents and other close encounters will often need to involve NATO countries, Japan, and other American allies as well as the USSR's allies. For the forces of each side's allies are often just as close, sometimes closer, and the potential may be just as great that an incident between them could trigger a superpower crisis.

"Hands off holsters." The existence of such agreements in no way removes the special need for the military forces of the superpowers to exercise great caution, as they do in time of crisis. During the Six-Day War of 1967, for instance, in the words of an American naval officer on the scene, the Soviet fleet was clearly "keeping their hands away from their holsters." The officer's vivid phrase captures a crisis control principle worth observing in almost every crisis.

During that war, Soviet vessels not occupied in routine shadowing of the U.S. Sixth Fleet remained in their anchorages. In this way, the Soviets signaled their desire not to become involved even though the Israelis were quickly destroying immense quantities of Soviet military equipment belonging to the Arabs.

President Kennedy acted in a similar fashion during the Cuban missile crisis, when he canceled American training flights in the direction of the Soviet Union and Cuba. In this and a number of other ways the superpowers can make clear to each other that they are not positioning themselves to strike. They can refrain from raising their state of alert beyond a certain level, or from evacuating their cities, or from interfering with the other side's capacity to observe the situation. They can deploy their naval task forces, and the accompanying air patrols, in a defensive configuration. Most obviously of all, they can refrain from direct military action, unlike the U.S. Navy during the Cuban missile crisis when it dropped warning depth charges on the other side's submarines. All these actions communicate clearly that "the hands are off the holsters," and that the other side need not act hastily in order to protect its security.

The Pentagon and the Soviet general staff could usefully generate a list of possible "hands-off-holsters" actions that both sides could take in time of crisis. Developed unilaterally, the list could then be discussed informally at the crisis control center so each side could come to understand better what actions the other would find particularly threatening in time of crisis.

Perhaps more vividly than any other safety procedure, "hands off holsters" embodies the rule of minimizing provocation in crisis. It can help keep the stakes limited, reduce uncertainty, and buy precious time for mutual consultation.

Safety Procedures for Regional Conflicts

Less straightforward but perhaps even more critical than safety procedures for close encounters are procedures for regional conflicts. One of the best examples of how a regional conflict can trigger an unwanted nuclear confrontation is the Middle East war of 1973. Neither superpower wanted the war to occur in the first place. The United States did not want its ally Israel to be attacked, and the Soviet Union did not want to be put in a position where it might have to intervene directly to bail out Egypt. Both Richard Nixon and Leonid Brezhnev were more interested in pursuing — and preserving — the new and precarious relationship of détente. Brezhnev went so far as to warn Nixon at a summit meeting four months earlier that a war in the Middle East was in the offing and that American diplomatic pressure on Israel was needed to stave it off.

Contrary to the superpowers' desires, however, war did break out. Contrary to their interests, it drew them into a serious confrontation. They partially lost control of the situation to their respective allies, who were far more concerned about their immediate conflict than about the risk of U.S.-Soviet escalation. The same situation could happen again today, not only in an Arab-Israeli war but also in wars between India and Pakistan, between North and South Korea, or in the Persian Gulf region.

Perhaps the most direct way that the United States and the Soviet Union can work to prevent regional conflict from igniting a global crisis involves their own communication. The natural tendency is to communicate less as hostility grows. In the nuclear age that tendency is too perilous. Communication needs to escalate right along with the conflict. This could be termed the rule of escalating communication.

The best time for Moscow and Washington to agree on ways to prevent a regional crisis from escalating is early on, before either side's interests have become too deeply engaged in the local situation. But there are limits to what they will, or can, do by themselves. They may be more likely to be able to agree on steps that *other* nations or individuals could take to help defuse the situation than to agree on steps they might take themselves. Here are three proposals for enhanced third-party involvement.

Regional congresses. In September 1979, Lord Carrington, the foreign minister of Great Britain, called together at Lancaster House in England all the major parties involved in the bitter civil war in Zimbabwe (Rhodesia), including the neighboring nations, the so-called Front Line States. The war carried a special danger because the Soviets were supporting one of the guerrilla factions. A lengthy process of negotiation had led up to the meeting. After weeks of tough talks, the parties finally agreed to decide the question through impartially supervised elections. In doing so, they ended a civil war that had taken twenty thousand lives. Whereas a similar colonial transition in nearby Angola provoked a U.S.-Soviet crisis that gravely weakened the relationship of détente, the Lancaster House conference succeeded in bringing about a settlement without acute U.S.-Soviet competition.

A congress in this context is a formal gathering of a given region's nations, both those immediately in conflict and those nearby that have an interest in helping to stabilize the situation. By working, at a minimum, toward an agreed set of ground rules limiting the conflict, and at best, toward its resolution, such a regional conference can help prevent runaway escalation as well as excessive involvement by outsiders.

In the nineteenth-century Concert of Europe it was common for the Great Powers, when confronted with a potential or actual international crisis, to postpone military action while their foreign ministers met in an ad hoc international congress. The explicit purpose of these congresses was not only to create a cooling-off period but to bring the principal parties together to attempt to find an agreed solution. Representatives of the nations immediately in conflict were present, of course, as were the representatives of other nations whose interest in the situation led them to counsel caution and moderation.

Clearly this institution does not translate directly into the circumstances of the late twentieth century. For one thing, once military events start escalating, it is hard to slow them down to the crawl required for implementing a full-scale international conference. But a congress can be valuable if it is held before major escalation starts, or conceivably after a war has reached a stalemate.

At the heart of a congress lies the attempt by third parties to mediate the regional conflict. A congress, however, can only be held infrequently and may, if a crisis is escalating rapidly, come too late. Needed in addition, therefore, is a permanent institution to carry on the mediation process.

International mediation service. Mediators help parties in conflict negotiate their differences to reach a peaceful agreement. They cannot dictate, only suggest. The agreement is often not a complete resolution but may suffice to stop either side from resorting to war. A skillful mediator helps the parties focus on their genuine interests and concerns, including their shared interests, and aids them in searching for a solution that satisfies those interests better than reaching no agreement would. This is what President Jimmy Carter did at Camp David in 1978 to help bring about the Egyptian-Israeli peace treaty.

Because it is easier to defer to a third party's suggestion than it is to back down to the opponent, conflicts are frequently settled by mediation. Indeed, institutions have been established in part to serve this purpose. Within the United States, for example, labor and management continually make use of the Federal Mediation and Conciliation Service to bring them together to talk when neither side wants to call for talks for fear of seeming weak. In international conflicts, too, a nation may welcome or at least accept proposals that it could not make itself, for fear of alienating some crucial constituency and of appearing weak.

Surprisingly, no organized body of international mediators currently exists that can provide these services on short notice at early stages of a conflict. The office of the UN secretary general does partially fulfill this function, but unfortunately it is constrained by many political considerations. In any case, the United Nations does not maintain a full-fledged mediation service. The modest cost of creating a regular, organized international mediation service, whether associated with or independent of the United Nations, could be borne by a consortium of nations. The service should be self-starting, able to offer its assistance in any given case without having to await the approval of other organizations.

A group of former heads of state, foreign ministers, and heads of international organizations with successful records of mediation could constitute a senior mediator corps. Since they would be drawn from around the world, at least one or two of them would be perceived as neutral in any given regional dispute. Appropriate individuals might include Pierre Trudeau, Kurt Waldheim, Jimmy Carter, Alva Myrdal, Alfonso Garcia Robles, Tommy Koh, and Willy Brandt. Once part of a senior mediator corps, individuals would be available on short notice, so they could be called on in the early stages of a crisis.

One significant obstacle to international mediation is that sometimes those who would be acceptable to the parties involved do not have sufficient regional knowledge and experience, whereas those who do may not have the legitimacy and prestige to be accepted. An international mediation service would solve this problem by combining both sets of qualities in a single mediation team. To be most effective, the senior mediators would work with professionally trained staff who are knowledgeable about the details of the conflict at hand and fluent in the local languages.

These considerations suggest the possibility of several regional support services. The standing staff of a regional service could monitor a developing conflict full time and be ready to brief the senior mediator when he or she arrives.

These staff people would have received professional training in mediation and other dispute-resolution methods. In the times between mediation efforts, their work in the regional service could include studying past crises, monitoring potential conflicts now simmering, analyzing hypothetical but plausible future crises, and participating in crisis simulations.

A rapid deployment peacekeeping force. If mediation fails and the regional conflict is on the verge of war, a rapid deployment peacekeeping force could prove valuable to head off superpower entry into the conflict. Imagine that a crisis erupts between Algeria and Morocco over their border area. The dispute has smoldered for years. Morocco is allied with the West, and Algeria has been friendly with the USSR. Oil reserves are in the area. Civilian rioting begins. Both sides call up their military forces. Tensions mount rapidly, but fighting has not yet broken out. American naval forces begin to move toward the area, ready to evacuate American civilians. Soviet vessels follow.

Within twenty-four hours, the rapid deployment peacekeeping force (RDPF) is ready to fly to the area. A standing neutral multinational force, armed only for self-defense, it does not contain any units drawn from NATO or the Warsaw Pact nations. Knowing this, Algeria and Morocco agree to accept the force in a neutral peacekeeping role. Arriving promptly in the border area, the force occupies a narrow buffer zone between the two sides. Its international legitimacy, the high political costs of attacking soldiers from so many nations, and its military power deter any attacks on it. This does not resolve the conflict, of course, but it buys valuable time for negotiations to begin, and it reduces the stakes and the uncertainties for both Morocco and Algeria.

A rapid deployment peacekeeping force would consist of military units supplied by nations other than the superpowers and their closest allies. Held in constant readiness, the

RDPF could intervene in trouble spots to stabilize the local military situation and facilitate negotiations. It could thus avert the military escalation that might threaten to draw in the superpowers.

Had a force been available in the Middle East war of 1973, it is conceivable that the first fragile cease-fires in the Sinai between the Israeli and Egyptian armies might have held. Egypt's president, Anwar el-Sadat, asked the United Nations to provide an international peacekeeping force. As it was, no force could be raised and transported in time. Both the first cease-fire on October 22 and the second on October 24 broke down, and the result was a nuclear confrontation between the superpowers.

Today it can take weeks for interested nations to agree on creating a peacekeeping force for a particular trouble spot, and more time to assemble the force itself. A standing multinational peacekeeping force, or one that could be assembled and transported on very short notice, could be dispatched before local hostilities even began.

Different forms of this idea have been discussed in United Nations circles. One version recommends that a thousand troops, two hundred from each of the five continents, be assembled and kept continually in readiness, as a "UN Guard." No troops from the superpowers would be employed. Cyprus has been mentioned as a possible headquarters and base for the UN Guard when it is not on active peacekeeping duty.

Superpower support for an RDPF, other than military forces themselves, could be helpful, even essential. Air transport, even of a relatively small force, is beyond the capability of most nations but would not be difficult for either superpower. The United States and the USSR could also provide other logistical support, communications equipment, and funding.

Ten times in the last thirty years, UN peacekeeping has

Watching for War. March 1973: United Nations Observers look out across an occupied Sinai. (AP/Wide World Photos)

helped stabilize a regional conflict — in such places as the Middle East, Kashmir, Cyprus, and southern Africa. In 1960, for instance, a UN peacekeeping force intervened in a Belgian Congo that was torn by civil strife and threatened by foreign meddling (much as present-day Lebanon has been), and it succeeded in keeping the country together.

Neutral peacekeeping forces have not always worked. Indeed, they raise serious problems, given the intense politics of the UN Security Council and of any multinational command structure. Yet the times when they have staved off war more than justify the expenditure of effort. The political crosscurrents can make success difficult, but where the United States and the Soviet Union share an interest in preventing a regional conflict from escalating out of control, an RDPF could work well. With such immensely high stakes in a nuclear crisis, the option seems well worth having.

Emergency Procedures for Freak Detonations

A third kind of spark, the freak detonation, is one for which emergency safety procedures are especially needed. A detonation may be very unlikely, but, should one occur, there might well be little time to act to prevent runaway escalation.

Suppose that a major East-West crisis erupts in the Balkans as a result of a governmental breakdown in Yugoslavia. The next day, too, an air battle between Pakistani and Soviet squadrons takes place over the border area between Pakistan and Soviet-occupied Afghanistan. Both sides lose planes. Immediately, U.S. naval forces in the Indian Ocean are put on full alert. About eighteen hours later, the U.S. Air Force Base in the Azores is suddenly destroyed by an atomic blast.

Is it an accident? American leaders ask themselves. Did an American weapon somehow blow up? Is it the work of terrorists? Is it some kind of Soviet trick? Or an attack by some other nation hostile to the United States?

If the Soviet Union was not responsible, it would have a strong interest in demonstrating this (to the extent possible) and in cooperating with the United States in trying to identify the true origin of the detonation. A number of procedures could help defuse this dangerous situation. Most of them are like the procedures described in the San Francisco scenario in the preceding chapter. In nearly *all* situations involving the detonation of a few weapons, a joint crisis control center could make it far easier to carry out these procedures.

But what if the Soviets *are* responsible for the blast, or may be? Despite many safeguards, an accidental launch of a missile is possible, especially in times of alert when some safeguards are removed. In this case, a high degree of restraint might be required to prevent a global holocaust from following rapidly. The same would be true if the situation were reversed, and the detonation occurred within the USSR. Tragic as this would be, there remains an enormous difference between the destruction one missile could cause and the devastation wrought by an all-out nuclear war.

In the precise moment when feelings of terror and rage might be driving the world rapidly toward war, time would be greatly needed for calm, careful deliberation. Before deciding to retaliate and risk a nuclear war, decision makers of the nation attacked might benefit from giving the other side's leaders a chance to provide critical information, and to establish, if possible, that the action had indeed been unintentional. Intense negotiation at this point might yield some mutually acceptable options that would defuse the crisis.

In a general way, each side has already committed itself to this. In the 1971 Accidents Agreement, the two sides said that they will immediately notify each other should a risk of nuclear war arise from an accidental, unauthorized, or unexplained nuclear explosion. Under the 1973 Prevention of Nuclear War Agreement, Washington and Moscow are required to "enter into urgent consultations" should the risk of nuclear war begin to arise.

The superpowers could build on these agreements and render them more specific. They could agree to consult and negotiate with each other in the event of one or a small number of accidental, unauthorized, or unexplained nuclear explosions. The agreement should specify that, at least for a certain period, the two sides would refrain from unilateral military action (other than a degree of alert) to allow for meaningful consultation. The United States could announce this as a unilateral policy of its own, even before reaching an agreement with the Soviet Union about it. Former Secretary of Defense Robert McNamara, who made a similar proposal to President Kennedy in the early 1960s, recently came forward again. No retaliation should be made, he argued, "until we could determine whether a reported attack was real or imagined and, if real, deliberate or accidental."

No crisis control measure is without its drawbacks, and this one is no exception. Perhaps the most obvious is the fear that the other side would, for some underhanded strategic purpose, launch a deliberate attack disguised as an accidental one and then proceed to use the consultation to provide misleading information on its intentions. A counterargument is that, regardless of any declared policy or agreement, such an attack would be far too risky for the nation carrying it out. It would mean placing one's nation at the mercy of the adversary's self-restraint at a moment of extreme provocation.

No agreement of this sort involving questions of national survival can be enforced. Its chief virtue is that it would further establish in everyone's minds the simple but critical principle that the most natural and important action that a head of state can take after a single nuclear detonation is to take time to reflect and to consult the counterpart on the other side.

Like other possible emergency safety procedures, a crisis consultation period is not foolproof. Just as fire safety procedures are not guarantees against small fires, so crisis control procedures are not guarantees against close encounters, regional conflicts, or freak detonations. Rather, each procedure is a small practical step that can help put out sparks long before they risk igniting a conflagration. Collectively, they can make a significant difference.

6

Cabinet-level Talks

Men are never so likely to settle a question rightly as when they discuss it freely.

Lord Macaulay, 1830

Even though both sides agree on the danger of unintended war, their leaders rarely meet to discuss how to reduce the risk. William Perry, undersecretary of defense between 1977 and 1981, reports, "During my four years in the Pentagon, I met with counterparts from almost every country in the world with a military capability, but neither I nor any other Pentagon official met with Russian military officials with one exception: on the occasion of the signing of the SALT II Treaty." This is not unusual. With Perry's one exception, the highest military leaders in each nation, responsible for controlling immense military machines in constant daily contact, have not met since World War II.

Imagine that twice a year, senior American and Soviet officials were to sit down together for a day to discuss crisis control. The U.S. secretaries of state and defense would participate, along with their Soviet counterparts, the Soviet foreign minister and minister of defense. Perhaps the chairman of the Joint Chiefs of Staff and his Soviet equivalent would join them. This is not an implausible idea. In a speech President Reagan gave in September 1984 at the United Nations, he in fact proposed holding regular cabinet-level talks, including defense ministers, on a wide range of shared concerns.

Such consultations could become the capstone of the entire crisis control system. Here the United States and the Soviet Union could reaffirm basic understandings, and review the development and operation of procedures and institutions.

These consultations need not be the usual endless talks, full of posturing and little progress. Competitive bargaining can be minimized when the interest is shared. For that reason, the Accidents Agreement and the Prevention of Nuclear War Agreement took relatively little time to negotiate compared to arms limitation measures. Negotiation over conflicting interests can go on elsewhere; the crisis control consultations would focus on the interest the superpowers have in common in avoiding a war neither of them intends.

The Incidents at Sea Agreement is a positive precedent. Its twice-yearly meetings have dual purposes: to examine any incidents that have occurred for the lessons that may be drawn from them, and to review the procedures in current use.

Why not extend this simple process, which goes on rain or shine, poor relations or good relations, to the entire crisis control system? Why not a periodic review with the same two purposes: to learn from past crises and to review the operation of the system, its institutions and procedures? And why not provide for an ad hoc meeting when a crisis seems to be approaching or is even already under way?

The consultations could take place at the crisis control

A Final Point. October 1973: Soviet Foreign Minister Andrei Gromyko, left, mentions a last point to U.S. Secretary of State Henry Kissinger as Kissinger prepares to leave Moscow after talks with Soviet leaders on bringing about a cease-fire in the Mideast War. (AP/Wide World Photos)

centers in Washington and Moscow, with the meetings alternating between the two centers. That would be an appropriate location to meet, since one purpose of the consultations would be to oversee the operation of the centers.

The participants in these discussions should be the same high officials who would play central roles in their government's decision-making process in the event of a crisis. In this way the chief "producers" of crisis control measures would also be the likely chief "consumers" of them. They would have the best sense of what procedures would be most useful. And they would have the greatest stake in using the measures, should a crisis occur.

The working officers of the centers could serve as staff for each consultation, preparing materials in advance and conducting briefings that day. They would report their progress in developing emergency procedures and in analyzing possible future dangers. And they could be assigned new responsibilities that emerged from the consultations.

Some of these tasks might arise from the review of dangerous incidents that had occurred over the previous six months. Suppose, for instance, that another civilian airliner is shot down. At the next consultation, the high-level officials might decide to re-examine existing procedures for preventing such incidents. They could assign this work to the center staff, requesting a report on the feasibility of an Incidents in the Air Agreement, and perhaps even a first draft of an agreement. The American and Soviet officers at the center would work not only with each other but with other officials in Washington and Moscow, and with other bodies such as the International Civil Aviation Organization. Six months later, at the next consultation, they would make their report.

The two sides might spin off some issues to a special working group. For instance, they might commission an ad hoc group to investigate the risk of both sides' computerized warning systems becoming unintentionally "hooked together" into an automatically escalating alert.

Requiring both the center staff and the spin-off negotiators to report back to the semiannual meeting of the high officials would offer an effective deadline, never more than six months away. It would also maintain a clear sense among all participants that any one question was merely a piece in a larger system. While major agreements would require approval from others in Washington and Moscow, the high officials involved in the consultations could themselves adopt and implement a wide range of helpful procedures.

Discussions could also center around ambiguities in each side's military stance. Currently, both the United States and the USSR are uncertain about the real meaning of various nuclear deployments and military actions of the other. Each could make inquiries and receive explanations at an authoritative level. Simply hearing what the other's concerns are about nuclear posture may carry great value. Indeed, in June 1984, President Reagan did propose to the Soviets the initiation of senior military-to-military contacts for just such purposes.

The consultations could also furnish an ideal setting for clarifying the global ground rules that the United States and the Soviet Union have gradually built up to limit their worldwide competition. Because these are mostly unwritten, they are open to conflicting interpretations. A case in point is Cuba.

During the Cuban missile crisis, Kennedy and Khrushchev reached a loose understanding that the Soviets would never place combat forces in Cuba that are capable of offensive operations. Still, much ambiguity remained about what exactly *offensive* meant. In 1979 a brief, and quite unnecessary, crisis occurred when the Carter administration suddenly "discovered" a Soviet combat brigade in Cuba and publicly demanded its withdrawal. Moscow pointed out, correctly, that thousands of Soviet troops had been in Cuba for many years to train Cuban forces. When U.S. intelligence searched for evidence that the brigade had the capability to fight outside Cuba and found none, Carter had no choice but to back off from the public confrontation. The "crisis" blew over — but not before doing considerable damage to the prospects for the SALT II agreements, just then being considered for ratification by the U.S. Senate.

Minor crises such as this one, as well as more serious ones, provide an opportunity for both sides to learn how to better prevent and control them. The period following a crisis represents an invaluable opportunity for learning. Memories are still fresh, anxieties are still vivid, and motivation to avoid a future confrontation is strong. If a crisis occurs, the next consultations could take up what lessons can be learned for improving the crisis control system.

The consultations might also serve as a valuable forum for superpower discussion of festering trouble spots worldwide. Conversation about ground rules will naturally shift from general principles to specific cases. In addition to discussing unintentional crises, such as accidental launches or terrorist attacks, they could talk about the Middle East, the Persian Gulf, and other world trouble spots with a view toward minimizing dangerous miscalculations. In a 1972 *Time* magazine article, participants in the Cuban missile crisis looked back at their experience and emphasized just this point:

> The Crisis could and should have been avoided. If we had done an earlier, stronger and clearer job of explaining our position on Soviet nuclear weapons in the Western Hemisphere, or if the Soviet government had more carefully assessed the evidence that did exist on this point, it is likely that the missiles would never have been sent to Cuba. *The importance of accurate mutual assessment of interests between the two superpowers is evident and continuous.*

In many ways, Washington and Moscow already appreciate the need for this kind of high-level conversation. Even in the depth of their strained relations in 1983 and 1984, the American ambassador in Moscow and the Soviet one in Washington held quiet talks with the other's foreign minister about the dangers of the Iran-Iraq war in the Persian Gulf.

Crisis control consultations would have one other important benefit. Should a crisis erupt, it might prove easier to control if the two sides' foreign and defense ministers already knew each other personally. High-level American officials who have played central roles in past crises have often remarked afterward that it would have helped them to have some personal sense of their counterparts. How will the other side receive a particular message? How should a message be worded to make its real intention evident? How should one interpret what they say? The consultations would help meet this need.

Consultations are not without certain risks. Discussions of ground rules, especially about specific hot spots, could generate misunderstandings, especially false confidence between the superpowers. This risk, however, applies to almost any communication on delicate questions involving potential confrontation. Still, the ministers would need to take great care in what they said and heard.

Consultations, moreover, could easily be misperceived as superpower collusion. Washington and Moscow would need to inform and consult their allies expeditiously, especially about discussions directly affecting their allies' interests.

Finally, the consultations could get bogged down in polemics and in propaganda shows designed to impress domestic constituencies and third parties more than to make genuine progress. Like some arms control talks, they might become an empty exercise or a political football, held when superpower relations are "normal" and broken off to show disapproval at times of tension when they may be most needed.

What can be done to protect the consultations against such dangers? The experience of the Incidents at Sea meetings and of the Standing Consultative Commission suggests keeping the meetings task-focused, confidential, small, and professional. To maximize candor about the most sensitive issues, it would help to limit the number of participants. One particularly successful NATO conference in 1974, for instance, assigned only one aide, plus translators, to each top minister. It might also help to set aside a portion of each meeting for informal talk off the record and without agenda. The best protection of all, of course, would be the participants' decision to keep the agenda focused on the shared interest in avoiding unintended war rather than on the two sides' differences and clashing foreign policies.

A crisis control system will never be complete, but it will steadily evolve in response to new dangers on the horizon. This will require a continuing dialogue. The single most important benefit of the consultations, then, might simply be to regularize, for both governments, the habit of high-level discussions of their greatest common interest.

7

A Briefing for the President

Bullfight critics ranked in rows
Crowd the enormous Plaza full;
But only one is there who knows —
And he's the man who fights the bull.

Domingo Ortega,
quoted by President
Kennedy during the
Cuban missile crisis

Just before eight o'clock in the morning on June 5, 1967, the telephone rang in Lyndon Johnson's bedroom at the White House. Secretary of Defense Robert McNamara was calling with a message never heard before by an American president. "Mr. President," he said, "the Hotline is up. The Soviet premier wants to speak with you." "Well," mumbled a groggy president, "what should I say?"

What should the president say? Think about it. The words may be the most important he will ever speak. The decisions that he alone can make in a time of crisis with the Soviet Union may determine the fate of American society, of Soviet society, and of much of the world besides.

Unlike almost every other judgment a president can make, there may be no second chance when the threat is nuclear war. The entire crisis management machinery needs to work right the first time. Like a moon shot, once the rocket goes up, everything must work correctly on the first flight. Unlike a rocket launch, the U.S.-Soviet crisis cannot be aborted and tried again on a better day. The most important decision the president will ever make may well come under circumstances that no one in Washington would have chosen.

Managing the delicate balance between defusing a nuclear crisis and protecting other vital national interests is surely one of the most difficult tasks imaginable. It requires the president to coordinate an immense and unwieldy political, diplomatic, and military machine under the most trying conditions of high threat and constricted time to decide. All the while, he has to deal with Soviet leaders whose minds are exceedingly hard to read, yet who could decide at any moment to destroy the United States.

Consider how you would feel if the next time you were in a plane, you were told that your pilot had been trained only in clear weather and had never been compelled to land in high wind. Piloting a nation through an acute nuclear crisis is no easier than landing an airplane in a storm. Yet the president receives little practice or preparation for this ultimate responsibility.

A Presidential Crisis Control Briefing

The American political system brings a new individual to the White House every four or eight years. How should the president be prepared? A body of knowledge about crisis management does exist. In part, it has been captured in the memoirs of participants in past crises and in the scholarly literature. In part, it lies as yet untapped in the minds of those who have participated in past crises.

A device needs to be found by which the president can acquire the accumulated wisdom and experience in crisis management of previous administrations. While no president wants to be told "how to do it," there are some simple, nonpartisan ways of learning the basic lessons that past crises have to teach.

Currently, on entering office the president receives a briefing on the nuclear options at his disposal; President Reagan in addition once observed a war game that pitted the United States against the Soviet Union in an acute confrontation over Central Europe. Even the idea of a crisis control briefing is not new. After the Cuban missile crisis, Walt Rostow and McGeorge Bundy decided to organize a "crisis game" for the president. A follow-up discussion would focus on possible crisis control measures. A date for the briefing was finally set for early December 1963; Kennedy's tragic death intervened.

In learning from past crises and in preparing how best to defuse a possible future crisis, what should a president learn?

Getting a Sense for Nuclear Crisis

"The strain and the hours without sleep were beginning to take their toll," records Robert Kennedy about the fourth day of the Cuban missile crisis. "However . . . those human weaknesses — impatience, fits of anger — are understandable. Each one of us was being asked to make a recommendation which would affect the future of all mankind, a recommendation which, if wrong and if accepted, could mean the destruction of the human race. That kind of pressure does strange things to a human being, even to brilliant, self-confident, mature, experienced men. For some it brings out characteristics and strengths that perhaps even they never knew they had, and for others the pressure is too overwhelming."

A nuclear crisis is a reality different from any other. The stakes are incomparably higher. The time is more constricted, the uncertainty more wearing. The situation changes hour by hour, minute by minute. The sheer amount of information pouring in, demanding attention and digestion, can easily overwhelm the decision maker. The press is clamoring for details or, worse yet, printing half-truths and falsehoods. Congress and allied leaders, feeling left out, are sending urgent messages, requesting an explanation and pressing for action. In the midst of all this, the president and the top advisers are trying to make the most difficult of decisions. Yet even the decisions they do make can easily go awry. As in the Cuban missile crisis, orders are misinterpreted or simply ignored, or extraneous events threaten to make meaningless any attempt at control.

As Robert Kennedy observed, people react in different ways to intense pressure. Some people, even the most apparently rational and calm, break under the strain. Reports of such behavior during crisis come from fires, emergency rooms, and sinking ships. It is a little like those days everyone has when everything seems to go wrong. At home, your children are sick and your spouse is furious. At work, a major contract, which you have been negotiating for months, is on the verge of falling through. Then, on the way to work, your car breaks down. You suddenly have the feeling that if *one more* thing goes wrong, you will lose it — your composure, your perspective, your everyday sanity. Obviously this state of mind can be extremely dangerous during a nuclear crisis. How can the president and the advisers protect themselves against it? How can they catch themselves before they succumb?

One way is simply to have experienced the pressure before, to recognize it, and to become more comfortable with it. Just as in a fire panic is the prime killer, so in a crisis our own reactions, our tendency to overreact, might be our worst enemy. Through recognizing the pattern of pressure, and learning our own limits, we can effectively control our own reactions. The goal, then, is to familiarize the president and the top staff with the sensations of nuclear crisis so that they will not be entirely new and unexpected.

Simply listening to others who have experienced such crises would help. It would help to hear Robert McNamara, a highly rational man, describe in a cracking voice how powerful were his emotions at the height of the Cuban missile crisis when it seemed genuinely possible that his and his colleagues' decisions, together with the Soviet decisions, might trigger nuclear catastrophe. It would help to hear descriptions of the moments of fatigue and anger, and the feelings of being buffeted about by new events: President Kennedy losing his cool over the Turkish missiles and yelling "Get those f—— missiles off the board."

Watching film clips from past crises — Berlin, Cuba, the Middle East — could help too. Films create a sense of reality that words alone cannot provide. How did these crises actually develop? How did decision makers respond? What did they actually say?

Perhaps the best method for creating a sense of reality is a psychologically realistic simulation of a nuclear crisis. To prepare physicians to give emergency care to a patient whose life is at stake, hospitals will sometimes organize a simulation. As the "patient" is wheeled in, smeared with blood-red paint and demanding immediate attention from the physician in training, a nurse says, "Doctor, your daughter is on the phone." A moment later, another nurse pops in the door and says, "Mrs. Jones wants to have her pain pills right now. Can she?" Almost at once the trainee hears himself being paged, and suddenly a piece of equipment he was starting to use malfunctions. This scene is a caricature, of course, but it effectively prepares a physician to cope with extraneous stress to avoid frenzy and fragmentation, and to go calmly and quickly about the business of saving the patient's life.

Imagine that a crisis "pressure cooker" could be devised

for the president. The regime in Iran collapses. The Communist party temporarily seizes power and calls for immediate help from Moscow. Suddenly, it is discovered that Soviet military units are starting to cross into northern Iran. American units are far from the scene, and must begin moving at once to have any hope of arriving in time to be effective. Urgent decisions are needed from the president. Are American forces to mobilize and start moving toward Iran? Does the United States issue an ultimatum to the Soviets to withdraw or face American military action? With every hour that passes, it will be harder for the Soviets to reverse themselves. Meanwhile, the press is shouting for a public statement. Congressional leaders are demanding an audience at the White House. The prime ministers of Great Britain and Italy are on the phone. Then, in the middle of everything, unconfirmed reports arrive of a collision in the Indian Ocean between an American frigate and a Soviet destroyer, with extensive loss of life.

Such a simulation would help the president develop some notion of personal strengths and limitations, and sharpen his psychological resilience to recover from mistakes, as well as his ability to step back occasionally from an overwhelming situation and regain some perspective. Perhaps most important, it might help the commander in chief sense the proper balance between the cautious humility needed to avoid a dangerous overestimation of his capacity for controlling the situation and the quiet self-confidence needed to exercise that control.

Developing a Game Plan for Crisis Control

An important lesson has emerged from emergency-care medicine: To cope with the overload, the stress, and the distraction, it is critical not only that the physician already have a feel for what it is like but that he also have in mind a game plan, a simple set of steps that he always follows in an emergency. The game plan allows the doctor to concentrate and avoid distraction.

A game plan is not a rigid plan of action but a useful checklist of steps to take immediately so as to buy time for a more sophisticated diagnosis and treatment of the case. In emergency medicine, the game plan is often known as ABC: Check the Airway, the Breathing, and the Circulation. A nuclear crisis calls for a game plan custom-fit to the president's own decision-making style, his strengths and limits, and the existing system for crisis policy setting. Each president needs to develop a customized version.

How could a briefing help the president develop such a plan? The recollections and reflections of people such as Henry Kissinger, Robert McNamara, McGeorge Bundy, and James Schlesinger, all of them experienced in crisis and its pitfalls, would be invaluable. The president should hear about how the existing crisis management system works and its strengths and weaknesses. How has the Hotline been used? For what has it proved effective? When will sending a letter or using diplomatic channels work better?

If the briefing gives the president ideas for how to handle a crisis, the crisis simulation provides the opportunity to try them out. The simulation affords the president the second chance that real life will never provide. Skilled and knowledgeable aides and experts would confront the president with a series of brief, realistic scenarios.

The president is seated at a desk, the "desk in the Oval Office." The phone rings. It is the national security adviser: "An immense explosion, possibly nuclear, has just blown up most of the harbor at Petropavlovsk, a Soviet naval base on the Pacific coast, not far from Japan. Important elements of the Soviet Pacific Fleet were in port at the time, and unquestionably have been destroyed. Photographic evidence of the extent of the damage will be following from U.S. reconnaissance satellites within about twenty minutes."

The president already knows, and now is reminded by the security adviser, that an American nuclear weapon is missing from the inventory of the U.S. Second Army, stationed in South Korea. Normally well guarded, it may have been stolen during a routine exercise in dispersing the weapons during an alert.

"Mr. President, what do you want to do?"

The president considers the options, thinking aloud. "What if I get ahold of the general secretary on the Hotline?"

A skilled questioner helps probe the president's logic. "What exactly would you say? If he accuses you of a dastardly attack on Petropavlovsk, claiming he had evidence of the bomb's American origin, how would you respond?"

The president decides to call the Second Army commander, played by an expert, to find out more about the missing bomb. He then consults his national security adviser, and eventually calls the Soviet general secretary, played by another expert, on the Hotline.

After going through a range of ways of dealing with the crisis, the president sits down and reviews what happened with his advisers and what lessons are to be learned. This might even entail playback of videotapes made of the simulation to underscore certain points. Through a series of such minigames, the president develops a usable game plan, a preliminary set of steps for dealing with any crisis.

Such a game plan may be as simple as running through the four key elements of a crisis and asking how one could deal with each one. How can I buy *time* for decision making? Should I keep the information quiet? How can I reduce the *stakes?* Should I take protective measures? How can I reduce the *uncertainty?* Should I reassure the other side that I have no intention of attacking? How can I increase my *options?* Shall I set up an advisory group and appoint a devil's advocate?

The game plan may begin by checking the information. Is this the full story? Or it may start by inviting a trusted friend in from the outside to help keep some perspective and remember the big picture. There are many possible game plans. The important point is that the president and the key advisers have a chance to develop and work with one that works for them.

Gaining a Close Knowledge of the Other Side

"The final lesson of the Cuban missile crisis," observed Robert Kennedy, "is the importance of placing ourselves in the other country's shoes." After all, it is their minds you are trying to influence in a crisis. It is they who have the power to destroy the United States and who have the power — with the United States — to terminate the crisis. A game plan by itself is insufficient. In a dance competition, it is important not just to know how to dance but also to know how to dance with your particular partner.

In the end, the decision for war or for peace will be made by a tiny group on each side. In past crises, American participants have often wished they knew more about their opposite numbers: What is going on in their heads? Through what lenses do they see reality? How do they react in time of crisis? A crisis control briefing should try to respond to these questions.

A professional basketball team will spend hours and hours, players and coaches together, studying videotapes of the other team. They will try to train themselves to anticipate how the other team will react on a level that the other team does not even understand themselves. If a basketball team

The Situation Room. October 1983: President Reagan is briefed on the developments in Lebanon. (Bill Fitz-Patrick/The White House)

will put in this effort to win a single game, surely it is worthwhile for the president and his advisers to do the same when the stakes are incomparably higher.

In preparation for the Middle East summit at Camp David in 1978, President Carter ordered psychological profiles of Menachem Begin, Israel's prime minister, and Anwar el-Sadat, Egypt's president. He and his aides studied these profiles intensively in formulating a mediation strategy most likely to produce a peace agreement. He credits his success in part to just such preparation.

So a crisis control briefing would profitably discuss the Soviets in detail: the people in charge, their areas of competence and incompetence, their world view, the way they make decisions in crises, their attitude toward high risks. The briefing would also dwell on the Soviet system of crisis decision making. How in the past have the Soviets responded in such situations? How cautious have they been? Not least important are the agreements in existence between the United States and the Soviet Union that bear on crisis behavior. How seriously have the Soviets taken the Hotline, the Accidents Agreement of 1971, and the Prevention of Nuclear War Agreement of 1973?

Simulations would complement the briefing on the Soviet angle. Soviet experts would role-play actual Soviet leaders and would invite the president to engage in dialogue so as to give him a sense of what it might be like to communicate in time of crisis with the Soviet leaders.

Planning Ahead to Prevent and Control Crises

The end of the crisis control briefing provides an ideal occasion for the president and the top aides to ask themselves the question that inspired this book: If we were now on the verge of a major crisis with the Soviet Union, what would we wish we had done or had talked about beforehand with our Soviet counterparts? What understandings or institutions or procedures would we want to have in place?

In emergency medical care, the key concept is *anticipatory planning.* This means figuring out in advance the kinds of crises that could possibly arise and the demands they will pose, and then preparing the necessary equipment, drugs, operating space, and trained personnel. As little as possible is left to chance.

With the help of knowledgeable experts and past crisis participants, the president can do some anticipatory planning, reviewing the kinds of crises that may occur in the future. The next crisis may not be a Cuban missile crisis; it might be a nuclear attack by a group of ruthless terrorists hoping to trigger a superpower war.

The discussion can then turn naturally to the needs such crises create — for immediate consultation to prevent misunderstanding, for the credible exchange of proofs that one's own armed forces were not responsible for the attack, for careful planning by military and diplomatic officers from both nations. The question then becomes: Can the existing system of institutions, understandings, and procedures be improved?

The aim would be to develop an agenda for action, a list of crisis control measures to study, to adopt, and to propose to the Soviets. Such an agenda would not be limited to steps for improved crisis management, but would include crisis prevention as well. No one can go through two days of intensive briefings and simulations of a nuclear crisis without emerging sobered by the experience and impressed by how all too easily things can go awry and a crisis can spiral out of control. The single most valuable lesson of the briefing may be that the best anticipatory plan for crises is to *prevent* them.

The Practical Details

Who, when, and how?

The president is not the only one who should participate. All those likely to be in the small select group that helps the president make the ultimate decisions should also be included: the secretaries of state and defense, the national security adviser, the vice-president, and others. The crisis control briefing will provide an occasion, perhaps the first, for all these individuals to work together as a team in a simulated crisis.

Perhaps the best time to hold the briefing is during the preinaugural period. Immediately upon inauguration, the president is plunged into the enormous responsibilities of office. While the preinaugural period is also a busy one, it is a time of preparation for the presidency. Ideally, the briefing would not end with the inauguration but continue with periodic refreshers and reviews of the game plan in the light of experience, at least once a year.

The briefing would have to remain private and confidential. In any simulation, moreover, the president-elect should not need to commit himself to a specific course of action that could compromise him in the eyes of advisers or anyone else. At any such decision point, the president can simply observe someone else playing "the president."

Presidential learning from the lessons of the past has good precedent. After the Bay of Pigs fiasco and shortly before the Cuban missile crisis, John Kennedy read Barbara Tuchman's account of the crisis that led up to World War I, *The Guns of August.* He was deeply impressed and disturbed. Although he had had little or no formal preparation for dealing with a nuclear crisis, the message of the book was fresh in his mind when the Cuban missile crisis broke on the world. During the ensuing thirteen days, Kennedy repeatedly hearkened back to the summer of 1914.

"He talked about the miscalculations of the Germans, the Russians, the Austrians, the French, and the British. They somehow seemed to tumble into war, he said, through stupidity, individual idiosyncrasies, misunderstandings, and personal complexes of inferiority and grandeur," his brother Robert later wrote.

On Saturday night, October 27, at the very height of the

crisis, he told his brother, "I am not going to follow a course which will allow anyone to write — if anyone is around to write after this — a comparable book about this time, *The Missiles of October.*"

The presidential crisis control briefing will help ensure that the next commander in chief who faces a nuclear crisis will be ready by design and not because of the chance reading of a book.

8

The Hard Case: What If the Other Side Wants to Win?

> Keep strong, if possible. In any case, keep cool. Have unlimited patience. Never corner an opponent, and always assist him to save his face. Put yourself in his shoes — so as to see things through his eyes. Avoid self-righteousness like the devil — nothing so self-blinding.
>
> B. H. Liddell Hart
> "Advice to Statesmen,"
> 1960

A crisis control center, agreed-upon procedures, and the like may all work well for handling an incident that neither side intended and for controlling a crisis that both want to bring speedily to an end. But in the ongoing conflict between the United States and the Soviet Union, crises are often not wholly unintended. Many crises begin with a deliberate action by one side. In 1948, for instance, the Russians cut off the railway and road connections between the Allied zone in the west of Germany and the city of Berlin. Fourteen years later, the Soviets sent nuclear missiles to Cuba. Whatever the precise goals in each of these cases, the Soviets initiated dangerous steps to advance their national interests as they saw them. They apparently assumed either that their action would not trigger a serious crisis or that, if a crisis occurred, the United States would very likely back down. Each step constituted a probe, a challenge, a gamble. How can a crisis control system help if one side seems intent on unilateral gain?

Leaders who face this kind of challenge typically see two choices, broadly speaking: accommodate or counterescalate. In July 1914, Austria escalated and Russia counterescalated; Germany and England followed suit. The result was an immense tragedy. It is perhaps not surprising that when Hitler marched into the Rhineland only twenty-two years later, France and England both chose accommodation. When he threatened to invade Czechoslovakia, they backed down again. "Peace for our time," announced British Prime Minister Neville Chamberlain upon returning from the Munich Conference in September 1938.

There are circumstances when accommodation works. When the other side's demand is quite limited, and not a step toward further aggression, accommodation can help defuse a crisis and prevent unnecessary conflict. In the negotiations of 1983 and 1984 between Britain and China over the future of Hong Kong, for example, Britain (in return for certain concessions) is essentially accommodating the Chinese demand that Hong Kong and associated territories be returned.

Counterescalation can also work, preserving important interests. President Truman's threat to use force in 1946 may have contributed to the Soviet decision to withdraw troops from northern Iran. President Kennedy's act of calling up some reserves in 1961 and reinforcing the American military presence in Germany may have encouraged the Soviets to lower their objectives, thus helping to defuse the most intense of all the Berlin crises. Yet counterescalation also carries dangers. If the other side does not back down but escalates even further, the crisis can lead to war. As in World War I, brinksmanship can sometimes lead both nations over the brink.

The Stabilization Strategy

Accommodation and escalation can each have strong disadvantages. There is an alternative, a way to defuse the crisis while at the same time protecting vital interests.

In the Berlin crisis of 1948, the choices for the West at first appeared stark: force an armed convoy through, or retreat from West Berlin with all the consequences this would entail for the political confidence of Western Europe, for the fate of the citizens of Berlin, and for American prestige. In Cuba in 1962, the choices at first appeared equally extreme: escalate by carrying out air strikes on Cuba, or do nothing beyond diplomatic protests on the assumption that the missiles only hastened by a few years a strategic reality that would have come about anyway. In both these cases, war was quite possible but was averted. At the same time, the United States successfully preserved its vital interests.

What happened? In 1948 the West began an airlift of food and supplies to the beleaguered citizens and Allied forces in West Berlin. Talks began in Moscow and Berlin. The West insisted on the rights of access to which all parties had originally agreed. Ultimately the Soviets relented and opened the routes to West Berlin.

In the Cuban missile crisis, Kennedy chose a naval quarantine and an ultimatum over an immediate air strike and engaged in intense personal negotiations with Khrushchev. The United States took the issue to the Organization of American States as well as to the United Nations. In the end Khrushchev agreed to withdraw the missiles.

These responses to the Soviet initiatives illustrate an approach different from either accommodation or escalation. It could be called the stabilization strategy.

The Berlin Airlift. June 1948: In an attempt to force the U.S. and its allies out of Berlin, Stalin blockades West Berlin, a city surrounded by Communist East Germany. The Western airlift of food and coal stalemated the Soviet military blockade. (AP/Wide World Photos)

This strategy begins with a certain way of understanding the situation. The other side's action, which triggers the crisis, is approached as if it were a dangerous miscalculation rather than an implacable step of aggression (something to which one could only yield or counterescalate). The goal of the stabilization strategy is to "persuade" the leaders on the other side to revise their calculation and change their behavior — not to impose a defeat on them.

This strategy is not appropriate for every crisis. It does not apply to the case where the other side, once having begun its action, is determined to carry through and win at almost any cost (although this is hard to imagine where there is a danger of nuclear war). The stabilization strategy is also not appropriate for leaders who themselves seek unilateral gains or want the other side to back down cold. It is a strategy for halting a crisis that began partly out of miscalculation, while protecting the vital national interests of both sides.

The strategy itself consists, in principle, of two steps: to stalemate the military action or threat, and simultaneously to open negotiations. To stalemate means to deny the other side any gains by arms, but without threatening the other side's security. The negotiations seek a resolution of the crisis. In short, the military path is barred as the diplomatic path is opened.

This strategy represents a significant part of what Truman did in 1948 and what Kennedy did in 1962. The Berlin airlift stalemated the Soviet military blockade. The talks in Moscow and Berlin expressed the Western allies' determination to maintain their rights, and helped prolong the decision time for months. Eventually, the Soviets realized the West could and would maintain its position indefinitely, and relented. In 1962, the quarantine helped neutralize the military threat, while the intense negotiations between the heads of state found a formula for ending the crisis.

The stabilization strategy deals with the four key factors in a crisis. Without requiring the defender to give in or back down, stalemating the military action gains time for decision and reduces the stakes (or at least prevents them from rising higher). Opening negotiations can decrease uncertainties about each side's intentions, and begins a process of creating options for defusing the confrontation.

The two steps of the stabilization strategy are essentially the two principles of crisis control discussed earlier —

minimizing provocation and maximizing consultations — adapted for a situation where the other side wants to win. Here, minimizing provocation implies halting the military challenge without threatening the other side's security. Maximizing consultations implies active, urgent negotiations to seek a resolution, while maintaining vital national interests.

Stalemating the military situation. The 1948 Berlin airlift succeeded in neutralizing the other side's military move — the blockade — without making any kind of military threat. The 1962 quarantine of Cuba also did not lead directly to combat. If Soviet ships carrying missiles stopped before arriving at the quarantine line, no fighting would occur. In both cases, the onus for crossing the threshold of violence passed back to the Soviets.

The object of stalemating is to balance the military configuration in a manner that neither tempts nor threatens the other side, so that both sides can then turn to negotiation to resolve the crisis. Both parts are important. The stalemating move must not be so weak that it tempts leaders on the other side to another quick escalation to overcome it. It also must not leave them feeling so threatened that they feel they *have* to counterescalate simply to defend themselves.

Land mines or naval mines, for instance, laid quickly across a legitimate boundary, can prevent the other side from making military moves across the line without directly threatening the other side's forces. A third-party peacekeeping force, interposed between the two sides and strong enough to keep them separated, can also work well. In some situations, such as the Berlin crisis of 1948, a move like an airlift can stymie the other side's military action without being threatening.

If a simple action to block or stymie is not possible, a less desirable variation on the stalemating move is to counter the other side's escalation militarily, although still without harming or seriously threatening the other side's forces. Kennedy's quarantine is one example: No Soviet ship would be threatened as long as it stopped. In 1983 the French did something similar. After Libya intervened in the civil war in Chad, the French dispatched troops and drew a line across Chad that the rebels, and their Libyan allies, could cross only at their own risk. But the French did nothing more. Paris sought to contain rather than punish Libya, to stalemate rather than to "win a victory."

Occasionally, stalemating may mean applying limited force to restore the situation as it existed just before the aggressive attack. In 1950, General Douglas MacArthur quickly pushed the attacking North Koreans back to their own border and achieved a stalemate. When, however, he went on into North Korean territory, heading toward the Chinese border, he abandoned all the advantages of a stalemate and provoked a massive Chinese intervention.

Any military action to counter a threat may easily be misinterpreted by the opponent as a bid for advantage. It is important to let the other side know that one's intent is only to stalemate. The action itself can be designed so as to make this plausible.

Opening negotiation. Stalemating is rarely an end in itself, however. Usually it is only the means by which the second half of the stabilization strategy, negotiation, can begin.

Henry Kissinger's talks with Leonid Brezhnev in Moscow in October 1973 produced a cease-fire between Egypt and Israel shortly thereafter; the follow-up disengagement talks kept the cease-fire from breaking down. The challenge in such negotiations is to find a way for both sides to back away from the crisis safely, without either side backing down. The parties need to look behind declared positions for underlying interests. Two basic concerns will especially need to be addressed: the interests in immediate security and the interests in credibility and prestige.

During the Cuban missile crisis, President Kennedy, according to his brother Robert, "kept stressing the fact that we [in the United States] would indeed have war if we placed the Soviet Union in a position she believed would adversely affect her national security or cause her such public humiliation that she lost the respect of her own people and countries around the globe." This led him to spend "more time trying to determine the effect of a particular course of action on Khrushchev or the Russians than on any other phase of what he was doing."

Each side's behavior in a crisis may pose threats to the other's security, even if that isn't the intent. At the height of the Cuban missile crisis, President Kennedy called a halt to low-level reconnaissance flights and night flights to drop flares over Cuba, for fear they might be mistaken for an attack. He wanted to reduce as much as possible any provocation that might trigger an unintended war.

Credibility interests often become as important as security interests. Neither side wants to be seen as losing. Neither wants its credibility in standing up for itself and its allies to be doubted by its opponent, or by neutrals or allies. By publicly declaring that the United States would not invade Cuba and by giving private reassurances that the United States intended to remove its missiles from Turkey, Kennedy made it easier for Khrushchev to withdraw his missiles even though neither declaration represented a change in U.S. policy. As the ancient Chinese military philosopher Sun-tzu said, "Build a golden bridge for a retreating foe."

Drawing on the power of legitimacy. Helping both oneself and the opponent to preserve credibility may not be easy. The rest of the world has something to offer that can help: legitimacy.

During the Cuban missile crisis, President Kennedy took great pains to legitimize his case and his actions. He selected the option of a quarantine in part because he believed it would appear more legitimate than an air strike. He also sought to mobilize those organizations that could grant legitimacy to the American effort to remove the missiles. At American urging, the Organization of American States met and passed a resolution calling on Moscow to withdraw its missiles from Cuba. The United States also sought international support at the United Nations.

"This diplomatic effort," his advisers later reflected, "and indeed our whole course of action were greatly reinforced by the fact that our position was squarely based on irrefutable evidence that the Soviet government was doing exactly what it had repeatedly denied that it would do. The support of our allies and the readiness of the Soviet government to draw back were heavily affected by the public demonstration of a Soviet course of conduct that simply could not be defended."

The power of legitimacy is central to both steps in the stabilization strategy, the stalemating and the negotiations. Many of the advantages of stalemating derive from the reality that neutralizing an attack, without attacking or threatening in return, will appear to everyone to be an especially legitimate act. And the negotiations will draw on recognized principles of international law as well as prior understandings and agreements in formulating an outcome both sides can accept. If the conflict is decided merely by whose will is stronger, eventually one side will have to back down. If neither does, war is almost inevitable. Legitimacy provides a basis on which negotiators can find an outcome other than a sheer test of wills. It helps allow the disputants to accept a resolution that otherwise may seem to be a setback.

Using the power of legitimacy means designing actions and presenting them so that they appear legitimate in the eyes of one's own people, of one's allies, of the world as a whole, and, importantly, in those of the other side. In a world of power politics, resorting to legitimacy is often treated as marginally useful at best. Yet doing so can sometimes be as critical to success as the force of arms. Without widely perceived legitimacy, it is difficult to maintain the domestic consensus and the allied support necessary to persevere in a military undertaking, as the United States learned painfully in Vietnam. In the middle of a crisis, one often needs the support of other nations, who may be swayed by international legitimacy. A case in point: Washington's success during the Cuban crisis in communicating its concern to the world community helped convince two standoffish African nations, Guinea and Senegal, to deny landing rights to Russian planes that might have flown atomic warheads into Cuba, bypassing the blockade.

Aiming to Tie

The stabilization strategy is designed for the hard case where the other side seeks a significant unilateral gain. Although the institutions and procedures of a crisis control system will work best for coping with the unintended element in crises, they can also be of use in implementing the stabilization strategy. Professionals at a joint center, for instance, could play a role in the intensive communication required to stalemate without escalating and to negotiate without accommodating.

In the South Pacific, the Trobriand Islanders have adopted the game of cricket — with one key difference in the rules. Since a loss by one rival village to another would inevitably lead to strained relations and violence, it is understood that neither side will be allowed to lose. The two sides play until a tie is reached. Something analogous needs to become the practice in acute crises, if they cannot be avoided altogether. The goal of the stabilization approach is to create a tie through stalemating the military situation and negotiating a way for each side to back away from the confrontation without backing down.

PART III

What Can Be Done?

9

But Will the Soviets Agree? And What About the Americans?

> If people do not show wisdom, then in the final analysis they will come to clash, like blind moles, and then reciprocal extermination will begin.
>
> Nikita Khrushchev
> October 1962

What About the Soviets?

For a crisis control system to work effectively, the Soviet Union must agree and cooperate. What are they likely to think about such a system? If they do agree, will they actually use the procedures and the institutions — or will they agree simply for the sake of propaganda? Even if they do use the system, will they also try to abuse it by gathering intelligence or misleading the United States in time of crisis?

No one apart from the Soviet leaders knows for certain the answers to these questions. It is even hard to know how American leaders will respond; but it is far more difficult to know this of a closed society, where policy formulation for national security takes place in strict secrecy. The best that can be done is to examine their record. What realistic grounds exist for supposing the Soviets might take crisis control seriously?

The Soviets' interest in preventing accidental nuclear war dates back to the very beginning of the nuclear balance of terror. They first proposed measures to reduce this risk in 1954, only a few years after they acquired nuclear weapons.

Soviet writings also came to express concern that another nation might deliberately draw the superpowers into a mutually annihilating nuclear war. In the 1960s and early 1970s Moscow made many secret overtures to Washington suggesting cooperation against third-party threats. Initially, these efforts probably had the primary motive of dealing with the Chinese nuclear capacity. In the late 1950s, the Soviets had become extremely unsettled by the cynical and cavalier way in which Mao Tse-tung spoke of nuclear war, accepting the possibility of losing millions of his own people to promote Communist goals. A *Pravda* article in the early 1960s contained a thinly veiled message to the Chinese, wryly noting that "the atomic bomb does not observe the class principle."

The Soviet concern about the danger of the Chinese provoking a nuclear war was a major factor behind the Soviet interest in détente with the United States in the early 1970s. This concern extended to other nations and to terrorist groups that might seek to gain by provoking a war between the United States and the USSR. In 1968, one prominent Soviet political scientist elaborated an agent provocateur scenario involving West Germany:

> The Federal Republic, having received a nuclear warhead, could, keeping it secret from the U.S., equip one of its vessels with a nuclear missile . . . Then it could send it close to the U.S. shores to carry out a strike against its territory in a manner suggesting that the attack came from a Soviet ship or submarine . . . The U.S. government, which would have to decide upon retaliation within minutes, might then order a nuclear strike against the USSR.

> Be it even a single missile striking one city . . . the USSR would inevitably have to retaliate. The adventurer's goals to provoke a major nuclear war would thus have been achieved.

In the early 1970s Soviet specialists began to lay increasing emphasis on crisis prevention and control, arguing that crisis situations represent "the *main* path by which the world may slip to global nuclear conflict." More recently, in a speech to American diplomats, Soviet ambassador Anatoly Dobrynin pointed to the decreasing probability of a premeditated nuclear attack, given the crushing retaliatory capability of both sides. He noted, however, "The possibility of a miscalculation or accident cannot be ruled out, particularly in such an explosive situation."

Soviet officials and specialists focus particularly on the danger that regional crises, such as in the Middle East, may become uncontrollable. At the Soviet Communist Party Congress in 1981, Leonid Brezhnev stressed the need "to take preventive measures to forestall" regional hot spots escalating out of control. Soviet specialists frequently write of the *nekontroliruemyi element* (the "uncontrollable element"), referring to the risk that small states may exacerbate a conflict, pushing the great powers to a dangerously high level of involvement.

In dealing with its concerns, Moscow has taken an active role in negotiating every U.S.-Soviet agreement relating to crisis control beginning with the Hotline. During the initial stage of the SALT process, the Soviets "pressed for an agreement in the field of accidents," in the words of the chief U.S. negotiator, Gerard Smith. Joint discussions rapidly yielded the 1971 Accidents Agreement. Later the USSR reached similar accords with the British and French. When the Non-Proliferation Treaty was being negotiated in the early 1970s, the Soviets made clear their strong concern about the dan-

Informal Summit. June 1973: President Nixon and Secretary General Brezhnev carrying on wide-ranging discussions in San Clemente, California. (White House Photo)

gers of nuclear weapons proliferating into the Third World. After they settled on terms, Moscow cooperated vigorously in lining up support around the world.

Perhaps the most credible sign, however, of Soviet concern about unintended war lies in their behavior in preventing and controlling actual crises. The Soviets were the first to use the Hotline to keep a crisis from escalating. In the early days of June 1967, they received information that the Americans were participating in the Israeli bombing raids that destroyed the air force of Egypt, a Soviet client state. Before reacting to such a direct attack, as they would have felt compelled to, Premier Kosygin used the Hotline to query the Americans.

Robert McNamara, secretary of defense at the time, recalls the moment: "The message that came through was essentially 'If you want war, you'll get war!' We were stunned. We told Kosygin that we had taken no part in the bombing raids. We told him to have his information checked. Thank God, however, that he had the wits to use the Hotline before reacting!"

The Soviets have also acted to head off a serious crisis before it occurred. On August 6, 1977, the chargé d'affaires of the Soviet embassy called the White House with an urgent and direct personal message from Leonid Brezhnev to Jimmy Carter. Soviet intelligence, Brezhnev wrote, had evidence that South Africa was planning a nuclear detonation in the Kalahari Desert. He requested American assistance to prevent it. A Soviet diplomat informed the White House later that day that a failure to avert the detonation "would have the most serious and far-reaching aftermaths for international peace and security." Moscow also later notified France, Great Britain, and Germany. With no diplomatic relations with South Africa and no influence there, the Soviets felt powerless to stop the detonation themselves. The superpowers shared a strong interest in preventing the South Africans from exploding a nuclear device. A successful test would set back dramatically the international efforts to contain nuclear proliferation.

President Carter, on vacation in Georgia when he received Brezhnev's message, returned immediately to the White House. American intelligence, initially caught unawares, confirmed the Soviet information. On August 15, Carter told Brezhnev that he was prepared to act to forestall the detonation. He sent Gerard Smith to Paris to speak with the French, who were supplying conventional weapons to South

Africa as well as their first nuclear power station. Jointly the Americans and the French issued a strong message to South Africa, demanding assurances from Pretoria that no test would take place.

Under this pressure, South African officials, who all along had called the accusations "wholly and totally unfounded," offered promises not to explode an atomic device for either military or peaceful purposes. At a news conference on August 23, seventeen days after Brezhnev's message, President Carter announced that South Africa had given assurances that "no nuclear explosive test will be taken . . . now or in the future."

A potentially serious crisis and a dangerous spiral in nuclear proliferation were averted. Without pressure from the outside, the South Africans might have detonated a bomb within weeks, according to U.S. officials. Without the Soviet tip-off and prodding, U.S. intelligence might not have discovered the preparations in time, and the pressure might not have materialized. As the *Washington Post* commented, "If this cooperation can be buttressed and extended — and if timely warning through intelligence is available in the future — what happened without much public notice in these past weeks may set a pattern of historic importance."

A few months after their tip-off about South Africa, Moscow again made efforts to control a potential crisis, this one of its own making. In early January 1978, both the Soviets and the Americans discovered that a Soviet reconnaissance satellite in outer space had begun to malfunction and was in danger of falling to earth. Worse, the satellite was powered by a nuclear reactor reportedly containing 100 pounds of uranium 235. If it crashed anywhere near a major city, the results could be disastrous. Although there was no risk of an explosion, the highly poisonous uranium might scatter over a wide area. When U.S. officials asked the Soviets for technical information about the satellite, Moscow, normally highly secretive, responded quickly. Fortunately, the satellite re-entered the atmosphere over a sparsely populated part of northwestern Canada.

The *New York Times* quoted an anonymous White House official as saying, "The real significance of this episode is that this was the first nuclear-related crisis in space, and it brought forth Soviet cooperation and informal preparations to deal with a potentially serious situation."

These three examples suggest that the Soviets will engage in crisis control and prevention, not just passively but actively, when it serves their interests to do so.

What Is the Soviet View Now?

Currently the Soviets have expressed suspicion about American motives in advancing crisis control as a subject for negotiations. In Soviet eyes, Washington may want to create a distraction from the issue of limiting nuclear weapons, which divides the USSR and the United States so deeply. Moscow suspects Washington of wanting a visible success on the crisis control front, as a way of diverting world public opinion from an American weapons build-up, which the Soviets believe world public opinion opposes. A *Pravda* article commenting on President Reagan's Berlin speech of November 1982 on reducing the risk of miscalculations asked rhetorically: "If a hundred MX missiles are complemented by ten telephones — red or blue — directly linking Moscow and Washington, will that make those missiles any less dangerous?"

The Soviets also express some skepticism about the substance of crisis control. They question whether a center, for instance, could be misused to make it easier for one side to escalate a low-level crisis. They suggest that the superpowers already have some crisis control procedures in the form of the Hotline and the 1971 and 1973 agreements; they are not yet convinced that more are needed. And they point out that mere technical improvements cannot make up for a hostile and dangerous overall relationship between the two superpowers.

At the same time the Soviets acknowledge that the superpowers share a true common interest in controlling crises. They say that further crisis control should be built on the foundation of existing agreements such as the Accidents Agreement and the Prevention of Nuclear War Agreement.

The positive side of the Soviet view of crisis control reached a high point when Vice-President George Bush visited Moscow in February 1984, to attend the funeral of Yuri Andropov. Bush met with the new general secretary, Konstantin Chernenko, and later quoted the Soviet leader as saying that there were two areas in particular in which the United States and the USSR could make progress: One was "safeguards against any inadvertent use of nuclear weapons" and the other was seeing to it "that regional conflicts do not get out of control." On March 2, 1984, Secretary Chernenko made a speech, little noticed in the West at the time, calling for emphasizing the importance of principles in preventing nuclear crises, and even "making them mandatory." Among the principles he proposed were: "to consider the prevention of nuclear war to be the principal goal of any power's foreign policy"; "not to allow situations fraught with the danger of nuclear conflict"; and "if such a danger arises, to hold urgent consultations to prevent a nuclear conflagration." Although these principles are not new, the fact that Chernenko chose to repeat them in a major address may suggest that awareness of the need for crisis control is growing in Moscow.

What Washington Is Doing for Crisis Control

Washington is also paying increased attention to crisis control. As popular concern has mounted about the possibility of a nuclear holocaust, as arms control efforts have stalled, as the likelihood of nuclear proliferation to the Third World has grown, government leaders in the United States have begun to put crisis control on the agenda.

In 1981 Senator Sam Nunn sent a formal query to the Strategic Air Command (SAC), asking among other questions how well the United States could recognize a "disguised third-country attack." This is another name for an agent provocateur attack, a nuclear strike with one or a handful of bombs that deceptively appears to have come from the Soviet Union. The answer from SAC: major improvements needed.

It was shortly thereafter that Nunn, Jackson, and Warner introduced their crisis center proposal. The senators suggested establishing a U.S.-Soviet joint center at a neutral site such as Geneva or Vienna. Staffed by working-level diplomatic and military officers from both superpowers, the center could help control any crisis that erupted and in the meantime monitor the spread of nuclear weapons.

In 1982, Senator Alan Cranston (D–California) urged that the United States and the Soviet Union station teams in each other's capitals, each of which could provide authoritative information to the opposing government in many kinds of crisis situations.

The Reagan administration responded with its own variations on the theme. In speeches in Berlin and Washington and at the United Nations, President Reagan proposed a new set of confidence-building measures. He announced that he was instructing U.S. arms control negotiators in Geneva to make three specific proposals: that the superpowers exchange detailed information about their military forces; that they continually provide each other with advance warning of missile test firings; and that they do the same for major military maneuvers anywhere. With this initiative from the president, and the backing of both Democratic and Republican senators, nuclear crisis control was visibly commanding bipartisan support.

Indeed, crisis control is one of those rare issues on which doves and hawks find that, to a considerable extent, they can agree. No one wants a crisis to get out of control. No one wants an inadvertent war. Although doves and hawks may disagree about policy for controlling and limiting nuclear weapons and about strategy toward the Soviet Union, they can agree on the imperative of controlling crises.

In the fall of 1982, Senators Nunn and Jackson offered an amendment to the act authorizing the Defense Department's budget, requiring a study by the department of the crisis control center as well as of an international "forum" for monitoring proliferation. Neither the administration nor the Pentagon opposed the amendment, and it passed without objection.

Secretary of Defense Weinberger responded with a report in April 1983. As an alternative, he recommended improving the Hotline by adding high-speed facsimile capability, so that maps and drawings could be transmitted. He also suggested setting up additional rapid communications links: one from the Pentagon direct to the Soviet military headquarters so that the highest-ranking military officers on both sides could communicate directly in a crisis; and one from each capital to its embassy in the other capital. In the summer of 1984, the Soviets agreed to the high-speed facsimile proposal. They were not receptive at the time to Secretary Weinberger's other suggestions, although they did show interest in the U.S. proposals for exchanging information about potential nuclear terrorists. Meanwhile, the Nunn-Warner center resolution was being passed unanimously in the Senate.

Unfortunately, the main U.S.-Soviet arms control talks broke down in November 1983, not over crisis control questions but over issues of the two sides' deployments in Europe of so-called Intermediate Nuclear Forces (INF). But some additional American proposals for further confidence-building measures to be taken in Europe were presented in January 1984 at separate talks that began in Stockholm. In June 1984, President Reagan reiterated his support for such measures in a speech he gave during his visit to Ireland.

Three months later, in a speech at the United Nations, Reagan stressed the need to "help avoid the regional conflicts that could contain the seeds of a world conflagration." He proposed institutionalizing regular cabinet-level meetings as well as "periodic consultations at policy level about regional problems . . . to help avoid miscalculation [and] reduce the potential risk of U.S.-Soviet confrontation."

These efforts by the United States government add up to valuable first steps beyond the Hotline. The agreement to enhance the Hotline, a crisis control measure, was the first measure to reduce the risk of nuclear war adopted by Washington and Moscow in a decade. Crisis control is one of the few areas where there exists not only a shared concern but also political will to make agreements. All the difficulties notwithstanding, American and Soviet interest in crisis control points to the genuine possibility of a full-fledged system for preventing unintended war. The time seems right.

10

Making Crisis Control a Reality: Lessons from the Hotline

To know and not to act is not to know.
Wang Yang-ming
(1472–1529)

Although crisis control may seem eminently sensible, the questions remain. How could it come about? Is there anything that we, as individuals, can do to see that it does?

At first look, the task appears overwhelming. It seems like a job for the government, far beyond the capacity of a private person to accomplish. There are too many people to consult and convince; there is too much inertia to overcome and too much effort needed over too long a time for too little a chance of success. What possible difference can one person make?

That first pessimistic reaction is understandable. However, in actuality, there exist few opportunities more promising for an individual who wants to help reduce the risk of nuclear war than the challenge of putting crisis control on the national political agenda. Perhaps the best way to show how the job could be done is simply to describe how it was done before.

The Story of the Hotline

It is the late 1950s. The cold war heats up in Berlin, Laos, the Congo, and Cuba. Anxiety in both East and West runs high. The United States and the USSR have been talking about disarmament; indeed, by 1961, they have spent "over fifteen years of unrequited labor" in the effort, according to U.S. negotiator Arthur Dean. Finally, in 1963, the first breakthrough is made: agreement on a direct communication link between heads of state for times of crisis. The Hotline is the first bilateral arms control agreement, the first hard evidence of a joint determination by both sides to prevent a nuclear catastrophe.

It was the governments that finally put the Hotline in place, but it was not government officials who started the process that culminated in the agreement. Credit belongs instead to two private citizens working independently of each other. The first, an economics professor at Harvard, found himself stimulated by a conference on surprise attack and by a popular novel called *Red Alert* (which later became the movie *Dr. Strangelove*). The second, a maverick magazine editor in New York City, chanced upon the idea in a phone conversation with a friend.

Thomas Schelling, the economist, says that it was not a question of inventing the Hotline but simply of realizing that such an elementary means of communication did not already exist. In trying to solve the problem of how each side could reassure the other that it was not about to launch an attack, he "discovered that nobody quite knew if we could get in touch with Mr. Khrushchev in a hurry. It was about then that more than one of us began to tumble to the fact that it was remarkable that there had been fantastic improvements in direct dialing in the United States but the president couldn't reach Mr. Khrushchev in a crisis."

Schelling confided his idea to a policy planner at the State Department, Henry Owen. Owen convinced Gerard Smith, then director of the department's policy planning staff, of the proposal's merits. Smith, in turn, argued vigorously for it with his colleagues in the Eisenhower administration, but made little headway. The Russians could not be trusted, opponents contended.

Meanwhile, one day in the fall of 1959, Jess Gorkin, editor of *Parade* magazine, was discussing the nuclear peril on the phone with a friend. Even an accidental launch, they speculated, could touch off a terrible holocaust if the side attacked assumed it was deliberate and retaliated in full. "Why aren't the president and the premier able to pick up the phone and stave off disaster?" exclaimed Gorkin.

When the conversation ended, Gorkin called a friend in the Pentagon and asked him to check out the idea. The general reported back that the proposal was both feasible and potentially useful. That was all Gorkin needed to hear. The campaign was on. Gorkin wrote an open letter in *Parade* to President Eisenhower and Premier Khrushchev, proposing an emergency communication link for preventing accidental nuclear war. "Must a world be lost for want of a telephone call?" he asked.

Parade's readers responded with enthusiasm. Thousands of calls and letters showed how deep public concern ran. Other newspapers across the country picked up the idea. The Soviet Union printed the letter in *Izvestia* and *Pravda,* the two leading newspapers, with favorable commentary.

Gorkin was not satisfied with simply publicizing the idea, however. He wanted to see it through. It was not going to be easy. Governmental inertia, the competition for the president's and premier's attention, bureaucratic resistance, and acute distrust between the two nations stood in the way, even if the two heads of state could be persuaded to view the proposal favorably. State Department officials worried about the president talking behind their backs to the Russians. And the chairman of the Joint Chiefs of Staff warned of Russian tricks. The John Birch Society launched a letter-writing campaign against the Hotline, claiming that "Washington is ideologically close enough to Moscow without making the White House a branch office of the Kremlin."

So Gorkin began his crusade. Throughout the summer of 1960, he tried to buttonhole the two presidential candidates, Richard Nixon and John F. Kennedy. Eventually they both made statements for *Parade* favoring the Hotline. Nixon wrote, "We cannot afford to close the door on any constructive suggestion." Kennedy did better, declaring, "It is vitally important that we have some method of instant communication with the Soviet Union."

Then, in the fall, Nikita Khrushchev came to the United Nations. Gorkin wangled his way into a receiving line for the premier. Thirty seconds with him was enough. "I grabbed his hand and kept pumping it," Gorkin recalls, "and asked him the question. He immediately replied, 'I am in favor of a direct telephone line between the Kremlin and the White House to prevent accidental war. It is an excellent idea!' "

After Kennedy became president, Gorkin obtained an appointment to ask him to follow up on his campaign statement on the Hotline. Kennedy promised to see what he could do. But the idea met opposition within the government and languished.

Gorkin persisted, however. Repeated articles picked up the theme in *Parade* and in newspapers around the world. From inside the government, his efforts were matched by those of Henry Owen, who had first broached the idea in the

Eisenhower administration. "Tenacious and persistent" and "a real professional," as Schelling calls him, Owen watched for every opportunity to advance the proposal.

Finally, the U.S. government accepted the idea. In April 1962, American negotiators proposed an emergency link to the Soviets at the Eighteen-Nation Conference on Disarmament in Geneva. In July, the Soviets responded positively and serious discussions began. Progress, however, was slow; the Hotline became entangled with the general disarmament proposals. An outside impetus was needed to clinch a separate agreement.

In October, the impetus came. The Cuban missile crisis convinced both Kennedy and Khrushchev more firmly than ever of the importance of direct personal communication. Relying on an ABC reporter to relay a message was frighteningly insufficient. Before Cuba, the Hotline was one proposal among many, seen by officials on both sides as secondary and treated as only part of a package. After Cuba, however, it became a practical necessity, singled out for separate negotiation.

Even so, reaching agreement proved difficult against the backdrop of the cold war and a fifteen-year stalemate in the negotiations. But the other nations at the disarmament talks prodded the U.S. and Soviet negotiators, reminding them of Cuba and urging them to take at least one step toward reducing the risk of nuclear war.

Finally, five months after the Cuban missile crisis and a year after the initial American proposal, the negotiators reached agreement. On August 31, 1963, the Hotline went into operation.

Today the Hotline is taken for granted as if it had always existed. It has become a part of the folklore, symbolized by the comforting if fanciful image of a red telephone on the president's desk. Better known than any other U.S.-Soviet

The Hotline. May 1983: The Washington terminal of the Washington-Moscow Direct Communications Link. (Department of Defense photo by R. D. Ward)

agreement, it speaks to each of us at a profoundly human level, one leader in the simple act of communicating to the other: "Let's talk it over."

Yet, as the story of its creation illustrates so vividly, the Hotline was not always in existence. Nor did it come about easily. Going beyond the Hotline is as great a challenge as was bringing it about. But just as the efforts for a Hotline eventually succeeded, so, too, can the efforts for a full crisis control system.

The foremost quality required for the establishment of the Hotline was individual initiative, the imagination and persistence of Thomas Schelling, Jess Gorkin, Gerard Smith, Henry Owen, and many others. They had the courage to step out of their given roles inside and outside the government and push vigorously for an idea they believed sensible and necessary. For some of them it took the willingness to be dismissed as foolish and impractical. As Jess Gorkin remembers, "One of the fellows in the office said to me, 'Who the hell do you think you are that you can make these people move?' And I said, 'Look, it isn't a question of who I am. We've got a good idea by the tail and I'm not going to let go.' "

Persistent individuals put the idea of the Hotline in the air. They created a political climate in which key actors in the government — the secretary of state, the secretary of defense, the president, and their Soviet counterparts — felt persuaded to make public commitments to the proposal. Gorkin talked the presidential candidates, Nixon and Kennedy, into putting their views on record. Owen persuaded Smith, who in turn convinced Secretary of State Christian Herter.

No individual, or group of individuals, however, can alone add a new item to the political agenda. It was not enough for Gorkin to write an open letter in *Parade* to the American and Soviet leaders. It also required thousands of responsive readers, each of whom took the initiative to write a letter or make a phone call. Hundreds of editors and writers at other newspapers around the world were needed to write an editorial or article on the Hotline. While Gorkin and Schelling could catalyze the initiative of others, in the end the Hotline resulted just as much from countless individual initiatives.

Even the commitments of the president and premier were

not enough. The Hotline proposal became bogged down in each side's bureaucracy and in the subsequent negotiations between them. Agreement required a further step: the proposal had to pass from an idea generally viewed with favor to one seen as an urgent practical necessity. This represented a significant shift, ultimately brought about by the deep shock of the Cuban missile crisis. Cuba generated the political will in the leadership and their respective constituencies, as well as among each side's allies and other nations, to bring the Hotline to the top of the agenda and act on it. No one wants to risk another such crisis in order to go beyond it.

How It Might Be Done Again

Those who want to put crisis control on the political agenda can capitalize on two distinctive strengths. First, crisis control is common ground. There is support for it across the spectrum, and little real opposition. Energy can go not into arguing and convincing but into moving forward. We have become so accustomed to fighting over nuclear issues that it may come as a relief to find an approach that can contribute to preventing a war on which we largely agree.

Second, crisis control is common sense. It doesn't require detailed knowledge of nuclear weapons, the arsenals on both sides, or the arcane world of nuclear strategy. Crisis control is readily understood because it is about people and making decisions. Everyone has had to make difficult decisions in a personal or professional crisis. Almost everyone can intuitively grasp how easily escalation can get out of control in a conflict, and how both sides must work, and work together, to prevent it.

For these reasons crisis control, perhaps more than any other step to prevent war, is a natural cause for private individuals and groups. People could begin by influencing those they know. Mainstream civic organizations could devote meetings to crisis control. Radio and TV stations could take it up as part of their public affairs programming. A community organization or a TV station could show a film with a nuclear scenario and follow it with a panel discussion about crisis control, involving local and state officials and citizen groups.

The possibilities are many for initiatives open to everyone. Schools all around America are experimenting with curricula intended to teach children about the problem of nuclear war. But at present, students often receive the impression that little can be done to avert a drift toward catastrophe. Adding the topic of crisis control would help counter this. High schools and colleges could also design crisis simulation exercises to help students understand the hazards of unintended war and grapple with possible solutions.

It is not hard for groups from different parts of a state to take the initiative to come together for a statewide conference. Because crisis control is common ground and common sense, such conferences need not be dominated by experts explaining the intricacies of weapons and strategy. Participants could work on drafting a resolution to be sent to their representatives in Washington, asking for action on crisis control. Or officials from the capital could be invited to the conference.

A group of citizens in the state of Washington did just this in the spring of 1984. They rented a ferry for a day, invited prominent state leaders across the political spectrum and from different walks of life, and obtained the cosponsorship of a Republican senator and Democratic congressman. In all, six members of Congress showed up to spend a day with their constituents, looking for common ground. What issue gained the most support? Crisis control. The congressional delegation returned to Capitol Hill with crisis control on their agenda for action.

Initiatives like this, repeated in different parts of the country, can have genuine political impact. Senators and representatives take notice quickly when an issue starts commanding broad-based support. Normally they find themselves being tugged in opposite directions on nuclear and foreign policy issues. They are left feeling uncertain; whichever way they vote they are bound to offend some of their constituents. But they receive a clear message when they attend a panel at which a liberal and a conservative, a freeze advocate and a retired military officer, all express support for one thing. This is the power of the "unlikely combination."

Local initiatives, multiplied across the nation, can start adding up to a climate of opinion. News media will take notice, and their reports will amplify the climate. Few outside the media professions realize how closely national news organizations pay attention to grassroots shifts in opinion. Polling, now highly scientific, never ceases. The large nationwide newspapers and chains systematically gather information about what local newspapers report, and national TV and radio networks observe the programming of their local affiliates.

As the media become more familiar with the crisis control approach, they will naturally start linking each new international crisis, be it a war in the Middle East or a serious collision between Soviet and American naval vessels, to the ongoing discussion of a crisis control system. Such repeated connections between events and policy proposals would keep political will aroused long enough for governmental action to follow. The sheer quantity of coverage would put crisis control into focus for millions and, in the end, would help make it a household term to people around the world.

A climate of opinion does not simply appear, or change for no reason. A new climate can be the result of a multitude of individual and local initiatives taken all across the nation and amplified by the media. Even then, public support may not be swiftly translated into action by the executive branch. But Congress can help.

The Powerful Role of Congress

In the 1980s, the impetus for a second generation of crisis control measures originated in Congress with Senators Nunn, Jackson, and Warner. Congressional action gives an issue a legitimacy and an aura of seriousness that little else can match. Congress can hold hearings, require executive branch reports, and publicize the results, often with dramatic impact. It may take only a committee, or an informal group of Congress members, or sometimes just one, to take the initiative.

A private approach often can prove effective. A quiet word to the president from several trusted senators on what their constituents are favoring sometimes has a bigger impact than even a unanimous resolution. A confidential message from the staff of a key congressional committee can carry significant weight in the internal bureaucratic disputes in the executive branch. Such support can be an invaluable aid to the Henry Owens and Gerard Smiths.

Congress can also carry forward, on its own initiative, the development of crisis control ideas. Congress has its own research center, including the Office of Technology Assessment (OTA). Currently none of the crisis control measures discussed here, including the joint center, has been designed in all its details; nor have competing plans been thoroughly evaluated. Much of this work could be done by the OTA.

The Importance of Worldwide Support

Would a crisis control system that went well beyond the Hotline be seen by the rest of the world as collusion between Washington and Moscow? This question, often raised by national security specialists, cannot be conclusively answered by any American. Only Europeans, Japanese, and citizens of other countries the world over can answer it finally, by demonstrating their strong support for measures to prevent unintended war.

The approval of pro-Western countries is not enough. Moscow pays attention to the opinions of neutrals, and to some extent to those of its allies. The power of the unlikely combination can make itself felt in world politics, too. If the foreign ministers of West Germany, Hungary, India, Mexico, and Mozambique all spoke in favor of an improved means to control crises, Moscow and Washington would take notice.

There are also major roles for other nations to play. Paris and London have hotlines to Moscow. Why shouldn't they, too, go beyond these? Moreover, nations other than the United States and the Soviet Union can assist with regional mediation, peacekeeping, and other measures to help contain and resolve regional conflicts. In fact, so hard is it for the superpowers to take initiatives in these directions without their motives seeming suspect, that some of the most significant initiatives may have to be taken by others. Superpower financial and technical support would then come upon request.

It Can Be Done

A climate of opinion built up by a multitude of initiatives within the United States, active help from Congress, and support from abroad can make it possible for the executive branch to act vigorously.

In the early 1960s, President Kennedy believed that there should be an end to the testing of nuclear weapons, especially in the open air. But he also had other goals he wanted to achieve, he faced political and bureaucratic opposition, and he knew he could not win everything. For a while, he was unconvinced that there was enough popular support for a test ban to enable him to achieve it, except at an extremely high price.

But more and more the public took up the issue. Citizens' groups began to speak out. Mothers began marching on Washington to draw attention to the mounting presence of strontium 90 in milk. Kennedy soon found that he could command enough support to act. The Limited Test Ban Treaty was signed in 1963, outlawing atmospheric nuclear testing — in great part the result of public pressure and citizen initiative.

Much of the support that crisis control needs has already begun to gather. Crisis control is an idea "in the air" now. The joint center has been endorsed by the Senate with no dissenters. Crisis control does not face any powerful opposition, in Washington or elsewhere. The main resistance may be sheer bureaucratic inertia of the sort that Henry Owen and others encountered, as well as the fact that during any given month, other topics seem higher on the national political agenda.

Those kinds of resistance can be overcome. The concerted persistent initiative of first a few, and then thousands of individual citizens, inside and outside government, serves to put the idea in the air and on the national political agenda. That creates a climate in which the key governmental actors can make commitments to the system and its various proposals. The national and international political will, fueled by existing deep-seated concern about the nuclear peril and recurrent mini-crises, makes the crisis control idea seem urgent, an idea to be seized and implemented now. Once realized, crisis control can pass into the national culture as a positive value evoked in school, on television, in movies, in family talk around the dinner table, and in politicians' speeches. It could become a national habit.

It can be done. The Hotline, and the principle that in a crisis the two national leaders should communicate directly with each other, has become a national and international symbol with bedrock popular support. Once it was controversial. Now we count on its being there. (Just think how people would react if the president announced that in retaliation for some Soviet action, he had cut the Hotline.) The proposed crisis control system can go through the same evolution. In the future people will count on its, too, being there to help prevent and defuse crises.

Who were the key actors in creating the Hotline? Who conceived it, supported it, created the political climate? It was not "the government," but people. The same applies to making crisis control a reality today. Individual initiative can make the difference. It is not up to "them." It is up to each of us.

Conclusion

There is a story of a man who left seventeen camels to his three sons. He left half the camels to his first son, a third to his second, and a ninth to the third. Despairing of their ability to negotiate a solution — because seventeen could not be divided by two or three or nine — the sons finally consulted a wise old man. After pondering the question, the old man announced, "I don't know if I can help you, but at least take my camel." That way, the sons had eighteen camels. The first son took his half — that made nine. The second took his third — six — and the third son took his ninth — two. Nine and six and two made seventeen. They had one camel left over. They gave it back to the old man.

Like the seventeen camels to be divided, the nuclear dilemma seems intractable. It sometimes provokes despair. But, looking at the problem from a fresh angle, as the wise old man did, we may hope to see ways out.

The danger of an unintended global war is the central political problem of our time. Like the passengers aboard Korean Air Lines flight 007, we are all passengers on a fragile craft vulnerable to the consequences of miscalculation, fear, miscommunication, and blunder. The innocent men, women, and children on KAL 007 had no idea what hit them. Neither might we.

Many have a sense that we are losing control over our fate.

As a thirty-eight-year-old multimillionaire who owns a football team and has given his name to a New York skyscraper recently exclaimed to a *New York Times* reporter, "The football thing is cute . . . Trump Tower . . . and all that: it's cute, but what does it all mean? What does it all mean when some wacko over in the Middle East can end the world with nuclear weapons?" In an age threatened by runaway escalation, even the American dream is accompanied by a nightmare.

Crisis control may be the beginning of a way out. It focuses not on the weapons, the "hardware," but on the "software" — the decision-making process. It deals with the most likely way war might occur: people making mistakes in a time of crisis. The approach is practical, and has not yet been thoroughly tried.

It also is politically feasible. Among liberals and conservatives, hawks and doves, crisis control provides common ground. Whatever else people disagree on, they can agree on this. No one under any circumstances wants an unintended nuclear war. A dangerous polarization has sprung up in the United States and Western Europe on the issue of how best to preserve our security, making it extremely difficult for our leaders and negotiators to deal consistently with the Soviet Union and the nuclear dilemma. As an issue all sides can rally around, crisis control could play a role in building a new and much-needed consensus in the United States and in the nations of Western Europe.

Between East and West, too, crisis control is potential common ground. It does not evoke the same fear of military inferiority that stymies arms talks. Once before, in 1963, the first crisis control measure, the Hotline, helped break an interminable stalemate in arms talks. Perhaps the feat could be repeated.

Crisis control is in no way a complete solution to the nuclear dilemma, but it is a key part. It can, moreover, buy precious time to implement other equally critical longer-term strategies such as reducing arms, increasing strategic stability, and building a safer relationship between the United States and the USSR.

Like the eighteenth camel, crisis control is both a fresh idea and one that was there all along. The most common reaction to the idea of a crisis control system is not "What a good idea!" but "Do you mean it doesn't already exist?" Just as people in 1960 were amazed to learn that the president and the premier had no reliable way of communicating directly and instantly in a time of crisis, so many today find it difficult to believe that the United States and the USSR do not have a reliable system for instant face-to-face consultations to avoid an unintended war.

Almost fifteen hundred years ago, in the legendary days of King Arthur, a society perished for lack of a pair of silver trumpets. We need not repeat its fate.

It is time to talk.

A Note on Approach and Sources

Endnotes

Index

A Note on Approach and Sources

The subject of international crises has attracted the interest of many political scientists, historians, and other scholars who have made contributions to its study, as well as the interest of many statesmen and public figures, some of whom have participated in crises themselves and have written about their experience and observations. The result by now is an immense literature that includes both scholarly books and articles and autobiographical and anecdotal material.

Two broad foci of interest emerge. One, served primarily by the scholarly community, is the social scientist's interest in understanding a social phenomenon. Though many scholars may hope that a better understanding will help lead to better ways of coping with crises, their primary goal is that of science: to gather a descriptive base, and to adduce hypotheses and theories that account for crisis behavior.

The other broad focus is on accomplishing as much improvement as possible, as rapidly as feasible, in methods for coping successfully with crises. This focus is served primarily by those whose interest is in policy. The hypotheses of social science represent one useful source to draw upon; others include newspaper accounts, historians' reconstructions, participants' memoirs, and so on.

This book falls within the second grouping. It is not a scholarly or scientific enterprise, but a direct effort to improve performance.

From the large literature on international crises, the following sources have proven especially helpful:

Allison, Graham T. *Essence of Decision: Explaining the Cuban Missile Crisis.* Boston: Little, Brown, 1971.

Blechman, Barry, and Douglas Hart. "The Political Utility of Nuclear Weapons: The 1973 Middle East Crisis," *International Security* 7 (1982): 132–56.

Frei, Daniel, ed. *International Crises and Crisis Management.* Westmead, U.K.: Gower Ltd., 1981.

———. *Risks of Unintentional Nuclear War.* Paris: United Nations Institute for Disarmament Research, 1982.

George, Alexander L., ed. *Managing U.S.-Soviet Rivalry: Problems of Crisis Prevention.* Boulder, Colo.: Westview Press, 1983.

Hermann, Charles F. *International Crises: Insights from Behavioral Research.* New York: Free Press, 1972.

Holsti, Ole. *Crisis, Escalation, War.* Montreal: McGill–Queens University Press, 1972.

Iklé, Fred C. *Every War Must End.* New York: Columbia University Press, 1971.

Jervis, Robert. *Perception and Misperception in International Politics.* Princeton: Princeton University Press, 1976.

Kennedy, Robert F. *Thirteen Days: A Memoir of the Cuban Missile Crisis.* New York: W. W. Norton, 1971.

Lebow, Richard. *Between War and Peace: The Nature of International Crisis.* Baltimore: Johns Hopkins University Press, 1981.

Lewis, John W., and Coit D. Blacker, eds. *Next Steps in the Creation of an Accidental Nuclear War Prevention Center.* Stanford: Center for International Security and Arms Control, 1983.

Nye, Joseph, Jr. "Restarting Arms Control," *Foreign Policy* 47 (1982): 98–113.

Roderick, Hilliard. *Avoiding Inadvertent War: Crisis Management.* Austin, Tex.: Lyndon B. Johnson School of Public Affairs, 1983.

Schelling, Thomas C. *The Strategy of Conflict.* Cambridge: Harvard University Press, 1960.

———. *Arms and Influence.* New Haven: Yale University Press, 1966.

Smoke, Richard. *War: Controlling Escalation.* Cambridge: Harvard University Press, 1977.

Williams, Phil. *Crisis Management: Confrontation and Diplomacy in the Nuclear Age.* New York: John Wiley & Sons, 1976.

Endnotes

PAGE

Epigraphs

vii "The greatest danger of war": Henry Kissinger quoted in Sheila Tobias, Peter Goudinoff, Stefan Leader, and Shelah Leader, *The People's Guide to National Defense* (New York: William Morrow, 1982), p. 11.

"There is no longer any such thing": Robert S. McNamara quoted in Coral Bell, *The Conventions of Crisis: A Study in Diplomatic Management* (London: Oxford University Press, 1971), p. 2.

Preface

xii The original report to the government: The report may be ordered for $10 from the Nuclear Negotiation Project, Pound Hall 513, Harvard Law School, Cambridge, Massachusetts 02138, USA.

Why Crisis Control?

3 "Every man, woman and child": Theodore C. Sorensen, *Kennedy* (New York: Harper & Row, 1965), p. 519.

5 "somewhere between one": Barton J. Bernstein, "The Week We Almost Went to War," *Bulletin of Atomic Scientists* 32, no. 2 (February 1976): 13.

"when the smell of burning": Ibid.

1. Sparks in the Tinderbox

15 *June 1948.* The Soviet Union blocks off: Avi Shlaim, *The United States and the Berlin Blockade, 1948–1949: A Study in Crisis Decision-Making* (Berkeley: University of California Press, 1983); Phil Williams, *Crisis Management: Confrontation and Di-*

PAGE

plomacy in the Nuclear Age (New York: John Wiley & Sons, 1976), p. 114; Hannes Adomeit, *Soviet Risk-Taking and Crisis Behavior: A Theoretical and Empirical Analysis* (London: George Allen & Unwin, 1982), p. 167.

"the abandonment of Berlin would mean": Daniel Yergin, *Shattered Peace: The Origins of the Cold War and the National Security State* (Boston: Houghton Mifflin, 1977), p. 377.

"We are going to stay": Lawrence S. Wittner, *Cold War America* (New York: Holt, Rinehart & Winston, 1978), p. 54.

but opt instead for a temporary airlift: Louis J. Halle, *The Cold War As History* (New York: Harper & Row, 1975), p. 164.

16 "the chances of war": Lucius Clay, *Decision in Germany* (New York: Doubleday, 1950), p. 367.

"at the brink": Gerhard Keiderling and Percy Stulz, *Berlin 1945–1968: Zur Geschichte der Hauptstadtder DDR und der selbständigen politischen Einheit Westberlin [Berlin: 1945–1968: On the History of the Capital of the GDR and the Autonomous Political Entity West Berlin]* (East Berlin: Dietz Verlag, 1970), p. 150; quoted in Adomeit, *Soviet Risk-Taking,* p. 75.

"if necessary": *Harry S Truman, Memoirs: Years of Trial and Hope, 1946–1953* (London: Hodder and Stoughton, 1956), p. 138. This is not, of course, a complete summary of Truman's strategy in 1948, which also included important economic pressures on East Germany and other actions.

June 1961: Adomeit, *Soviet Risk-Taking,* pp. 203–11.

In late October: Ibid., pp. 214–15.

17 American diplomats continue to enter: Sorenson, *Kennedy,* p. 595.

Employees of the Soviet consulate: Robert F. Kennedy, *Thirteen Days: A Memoir of the Cuban Missile Crisis* (New York: W. W. Norton, 1971), p. 71.

Kennedy's advisers have decided earlier: Graham T. Allison, *Essence of Decision: Explaining the Cuban Missile Crisis* (Boston: Little, Brown, 1971), p. 225.

An American U-2 is shot down: Ibid., p. 75.

"in an entirely": Ibid., p. 90.

Secretary of Defense Robert S. McNamara looks: Elie Abel, *The Missile Crisis* (Philadelphia: J. B. Lippincott, 1968), p. 203.

Instead he increases diplomatic pressure: Kennedy, *Thirteen Days,* p. 71.

PAGE

19 "Kosygin said": Lyndon Baines Johnson, *The Vantage Point: Perspectives of the Presidency* (New York: Holt, Rinehart & Winston, 1971), p. 302.

20 "gravest consequences": Scott Sagan, "Lessons of the Yom Kippur Alert," *Foreign Policy* 36 (Fall 1979): 168.
"I will say it straight": Ibid.
"Incalculable consequences": Barry M. Blechman, "The Political Utility of Nuclear Weapons," *International Security* 7, no. 1 (Summer 1982): 141.
"a smoldering fuse": *Pravda,* 28 November 1958; quoted in Adomeit, *Soviet Risk-Taking,* p. 288.

21 "A trigger-happy Russian pilot": Truman, *Memoirs,* p. 149.

22 "For seventy tense minutes": Johnson, *Vantage Point,* p. 300.
"thought the *Liberty*": "Sect. Rusk and Sect. of Defense McNamara Discuss Vietnam and Korea on 'Meet the Press,'" *Department of State Bulletin* 63, no. 1496 (26 February 1968): 271; quoted in Jonathan Trumbull Howe, *Multi-crises: Sea Power and Global Politics in the Missile Age* (Cambridge: MIT Press, 1971), pp. 102–3.
Johnson ordered carrier planes: Johnson, *Vantage Point,* pp. 300–301.

23 "Thank goodness": Ibid.
"the *Gato* prepared for action": United Press International report published in the *Indianapolis Star,* 16 February 1976.
"There's always some": Allison, *Essence,* p. 141.
When such suspicious events: Paul Bracken, *The Command and Control of Nuclear Forces* (New Haven: Yale University Press, 1983), pp. 59–65.

25 Libya sought unsuccessfully to buy a bomb: Steve Weissman, *The Islamic Bomb* (New York: Times Books, 1981), p. 64.

26 In 1974 the Boston police received: "In Atom-bomb Scare, Federal NEST Team Flies to the Rescue," *Wall Street Journal,* 21 October 1980.

27 During World War II: Leo Szilard, *The Voice of the Dolphins and Other Stories* (New York: Simon & Schuster, 1941), p. 49n.
Richard Nixon recalls that: Jess Gorkin, "World Leaders Agree on Parade's Telephone Line," *Parade,* 30 October 1960, p. 6.
A couple of years later: Stockholm International Peace Research Institute, *Yearbook of World Armaments and Disarmaments* 2 (London: Duckworth, 1969): 261.

PAGE

"The complexity of the system": Bracken, *Command and Control,* p. 53.

28 "It's the oldest principle of war": Ibid. pp. 228–29. Additional safeguards have been instituted since the early 1960s, when this interview took place. Nevertheless, we cannot be 100 percent certain that control over the thousands of deployed weapons would be perfect during a time of crisis.

29 "The headquarters of the U.S. military command": Ibid. p. 66.

2. Runaway Escalation

31 "It isn't the first step": Kennedy, *Thirteen Days,* p. 76.

34 ". . . I cannot agree": Max Montgelas and Walter Schuking, eds., *Outbreak of the World War: German Documents Collected by Karl Kautsky* (New York: Oxford University Press, 1924), p. 390.

"In view of": Ibid., p. 433.

"Your majesty"; "it cannot be done": Barbara Tuchman, *The Guns of August* (New York: Macmillan, 1962), p. 99.

35 But behind these particulars: The author wishes to acknowledge Roger Fisher for his elegant development of the ideas of high stakes, short time, and high uncertainty as core features of a crisis. To these I have added the notion of few apparent or usable options.

36 He thought that Israel would accept: Mohammed Heikal, *The Cairo Documents* (New York: Doubleday, 1973), p. 241.

37 There is a story, possibly apocryphal: During the autumn there were various other indications as well that the Kremlin would not treat the December deadline as rigid. The sense of crisis in the West lessened in stages, not all at once.

"much to our own surprise": *Boston Globe,* 30 October 1983.

38 On October 22: Blechman, "The Political Utility," p. 137.

In their memoirs: Richard Nixon, *RN: The Memoirs of Richard Nixon* (New York: Grosset & Dunlap, 1978), p. 885; Henry Kissinger, *Years of Upheaval* (Boston: Little, Brown, 1982), p. 298.

40 This strategy, known as a "commitment strategy": Thomas Schelling, *A Strategy of Conflict* (Cambridge: Harvard University Press, 1960), p. 21.

Researchers have shown that people under stress tend to focus:

PAGE

There is an extensive corpus of social science literature dedicated to crisis stress and its effects. One good introduction to its application to international crises is: Ole Holsti, *Crisis, Escalation, War* (Montreal: McGill–Queens University Press, 1972); within this work see especially the article by Alexander George, "The Case for Multiple Advocacy."

42 But the spiral of escalation: The description of escalation presented in this chapter is not intended as a full analysis of how escalation occurs in crisis or war. It is a simplified description, sufficient for the purposes of this book. For an in-depth analysis of escalation processes see: Richard Smoke, *War: Controlling Escalation* (Cambridge: Harvard University Press, 1977).

"How did it happen?"; "Ah, if only": Ole R. Holsti, "Perception and Action in the 1914 Crisis," in J. David Singer, *Quantitative International Politics* (New York: Free Press, 1968), p. 134n.

3. Beyond the Hotline

45 "The notion of a control system": Henry Kissinger, *The Necessity for Choice* (New York: Harper and Brothers, 1961), p. 229.

"I think these few minutes"; "Was the world on the brink": Kennedy, *Thirteen Days,* pp. 69–71.

46 For almost twenty years before 1814: Paul Gordon Lauren, "Crisis Prevention in 19th Century Diplomacy," in Alexander George, ed., *Managing U.S.-Soviet Rivalry: Problems of Crisis Prevention* (Boulder, Colo.: Westview Press, 1983).

"only collective action": Ibid., p. 32.

47 "an epoch of": Ibid., p. 33.

48 "There is no longer": Bell, *Conventions of Crisis*, p. 2.

"What guided all"; "was an effort": Kennedy, *Thirteen Days,* p. 102.

49 "We were not going to misjudge": Ibid., pp. 40–41.

50 "If you have not lost": Ibid., p. 67.

51 If the Cuban missile crisis: Richard N. Lebow, *Between Peace and War: The Nature of International Crisis* (Baltimore: Johns Hopkins University Press, 1981), p. 3.

52 "to act in such a way": United States Arms Control and Disarmament Agency, *Arms Control and Disarmament Agreements: Texts and Histories of Negotiations* (Washington, D.C.: Government Printing Office, 1980), p. 112.

PAGE

4. A Joint Crisis Control Center

62 It was a later version: *New York Times,* 16 June 1984, p. B-5.
Earlier that year: In his April 1983 report, Secretary Weinberger concludes that it would not be desirable to establish a joint crisis control center at this time. He adds, however, "Over time, our experience with operating a Joint Military Communications Link might allow us to pursue the idea of a crisis control center."

The specific design of a center suggested in the next paragraph and later in this chapter is merely illustrative. A final plan would require substantial analysis and design work in Washington and Moscow, as well, of course, as negotiation between them.

64 In the San Francisco scenario: Under current arrangements, the Standing Consultative Commission (SCC) has responsibility for authenticating that accidental or unauthorized launches are indeed accidental or unauthorized. That responsibility would need to be transferred to the joint crisis control center. Or it might be shared, with the center providing initial verification and the SCC responsible for later follow-up.

69 Such close work during normal times: A small staff could not itself cope with the details of all possible contingencies, of course. But it could have worked ahead of time on how to tap the expertise scattered through both governments, on how to bring together detailed information from two very different systems, and on how to coordinate implementation.
Called the Standing Consultative Commission: Sydney Graybeal, "Negotiating an Accident Prevention Center: The Experience of the Standing Consultative Commission," in *Next Steps to the Creation of an Accidental Nuclear War Prevention Center,* ed. John W. Lewis and Coit D. Blacker (Stanford: Center for International Security and Arms Control, 1983), pp. 25–38.

70 According to Ambassador Sydney Graybeal: Ibid., p. 26.
The crisis control center could start out: I do not mean to imply that the functions of the SCC and a joint center are so similar that the SCC experience provides a high level of confidence that all problems can be readily solved. There are significant differences in the two sets of functions. But the SCC experience provides a reasonable basis for hope that an imaginative approach and careful design could yield adequate safeguards for a center with limited functions.

PAGE

72 "To work together in these areas": *Atlanta Constitution,* 17 November 1982.

Twenty years after the center is established: This chapter does not attempt to provide a detailed evaluation of the design or specific missions of a joint crisis control center. As of this writing, the most thorough such evaluation available appears in Lewis, ed., *Next Steps;* other useful discussions of the joint center concept are: Richard K. Betts, "A Joint Nuclear Risk Control Center" (Washington, D.C.: Brookings Institution, 1983); Barry M. Blechman, "U.S.-Soviet Nuclear Risk Management Centers," in *Avoiding Inadvertent War: Crisis Management,* ed. Hilliard Roderick (Austin, Tex.: Lyndon B. Johnson School of Public Affairs, 1983), pp. 78–88; and William L. Ury and Richard Smoke, *Beyond the Hotline: Controlling a Nuclear Crisis (A Report to the United States Arms Control and Disarmament Agency)* (Cambridge: Harvard Law School Nuclear Negotiation Project, 1984).

5. Emergency Safety Procedures

77 Admiral Elmo Zumwalt, later the highest-ranking: Elmo R. Zumwalt, *On Watch: A Memoir* (New York: Quadrangle, 1976), p. 391.

79 "The question is, Mr. President": David L. Larson, ed., *The "Cuban Crisis" of 1962: Selected Documents and Chronology* (Boston: Houghton Mifflin, 1963), p. 164.

Or army helicopters, patrolling the ground: *New York Times,* 21 April 1984, p. A-1.

80 in the words of an American naval officer: personal communication to the author.

83 In September 1979, Lord Carrington: Larry C. Napper, "The African Terrain and U.S.-Soviet Conflict," in George, ed., *Managing U.S.-Soviet Rivalry,* p. 169.

90 "enter into urgent": Arms Control and Disarmament Agency, *Arms Control,* p. 160.

91 "until we could determine": Robert S. McNamara, "No Second Use — Until," *New York Times,* 2 February 1983, p. A-19.

6. Cabinet-level Talks

93 Men are never so likely: Lord Macaulay quoted in Robert Southey, *Colloquies on Society* (New York: Cassell and Co. Ltd., 1887).

PAGE

"during my four years": William Perry, "Measures to Reduce the Risk of Nuclear War," in Lewis, ed., *Next Steps,* p. 23.
With Perry's one exception: "Fact Sheet: U.S.-Soviet Bilateral Relations" (press release from the Office of the Press Secretary, the White House), 27 June 1984, p. 4.

98 "The Crisis could and should": Dean Rusk, Robert McNamara, George W. Ball, Roswell L. Gilpatric, Theodore Sorensen, and McGeorge Bundy, "Lessons of the Cuban Missile Crisis," *Time,* 27 September 1972, p. 85.

7. A Briefing for the President

101 Bullfight critics ranked in rows: a poem by Domingo Ortega as translated by Robert Graves, in Robert Graves, *Oxford Addresses on Poetry* (New York: Doubleday, 1962).
"Mr. President"; "the Hotline": Johnson, *Vantage Point,* p. 289.
"Well"; "What should": personal communication to the author from Robert S. McNamara.

103 Currently, on entering office: "Reagan as Military Commander," *New York Times Magazine,* 15 January 1984.
"The strain and the hours"; "However . . . those human weaknesses": Kennedy, *Thirteen Days,* p. 22.

105 "Get those f——": Allison, *Essence,* p. 142.

109 "The final lesson of the Cuban missile crisis": Kennedy, *Thirteen Days,* p. 100.

111 He credits his success: Jimmy Carter, *Keeping the Faith: Memoirs of a President* (New York: Bantam, 1982), p. 320.

113 He was deeply impressed; "He talked about": Kennedy, *Thirteen Days,* p. 40.

114 "I am not going to follow": Ibid., p. 105.

8. The Hard Case: What If the Other Side Wants to Win?

115 Keep strong, if possible.: B. H. Liddell Hart, *Deterrent or Defence: A Fresh Look at the West's Military Position* (London: Stevens and Sons, 1960), pp. 247–48.

117 It could be called: The term "strategy" is used here in its general meaning, not as experts might use it. From the specialist's viewpoint, it might be better termed an approach, which could be supported by various strategies and tactics depending upon the circumstances.

PAGE

121 Paris sought to contain: Piero Gleijeses, "French Skill on Chad," *New York Times,* 29 August 1983, p. A-19.
Henry Kissinger's talks: Alexander L. George, "The Arab-Israeli War of 1973," in George, ed., *Managing U.S.-Soviet Rivalry,* p. 140.

122 "kept stressing the fact"; "more time trying": Kennedy, *Thirteen Days,* p. 126.

123 During the Cuban missile crisis: Allison, *Essence,* p. 140.
"This diplomatic effort": Rusk et al., "Lessons of the Cuban Missile Crisis, p. 86.

9. But Will the Soviets Agree? And What About the Americans?

129 "If people do not show wisdom": Kennedy, *Thirteen Days,* p. 67.

130 "the atomic bomb does not observe": *Pravda,* 14 July 1963; quoted in W. Zimmerman, *Soviet Perspectives on International Relations 1956–67* (Princeton: Princeton University Press, 1969), p. 5.
The Soviet concern about the danger: In the SALT I negotiations the Soviets tried to work in a statement against "third parties," which clearly was aimed against China.
"The Federal Republic, having received": H. A. Trofimenko, *The Strategy of Global War* (Moscow, 1968), p. 229, as cited in Adam B. Ulam, *Dangerous Relations* (New York: Oxford University Press, 1983), pp. 49–50.

131 "the *main* path": V. Zhurkin and E. Primakov, *Mezhdunarodnye Konflikty* (Moscow: Izd-vo Mezhdunarodnye otnosheniia, 1972), p. 19; emphasis added.
"The possibility of a miscalculation": *New York Times Magazine,* 13 May 1984, p. 26.
"to take preventive measures": *Materialy XXVI s"ezda KPSS* (Moscow, 1981), p. 28.
Soviet specialists frequently write: Zhurkin, *Mezhdunarodnye,* p. 20.
"pressed for an agreement": Gerard Smith, *Double Talk: The Story of the First Strategic Limitations Talks* (New York: Doubleday, 1980), p. 283.

132 The Soviets were the first: Johnson, *Vantage Point,* p. 289.

133 "The message that came through": personal communication to the author from Robert S. McNamara.

PAGE

On August 6, 1977: *Washington Post,* 28 August 1977.
"would have the most serious": Ibid.

134 "wholly and totally": Ibid.
"no nuclear explosive test": Ibid.
"If this cooperation can be buttressed": Ibid.

135 "The real significance of this episode": *New York Times,* 25 January 1978, pp. A-1, 11.

135 "If a hundred MX missiles": *Pravda,* 25 November 1982. Recent Soviet statements expressing wariness about nuclear crisis control must also be evaluated in light of the Soviet campaign against the deployment of Pershing II missiles in Europe. In the fall of 1983, Marshal Viktor Kulikov expressed concern over the short warning time of the Pershing IIs, asserting that it "would make it practically impossible to prevent a conflict resulting from an error or technical fault" (*New York Times,* 14 October 1983). Against the background of these Soviet concerns, American proposals for nuclear crisis control seem invidious: The major Soviet objective was to stop deployment, not to reduce the risk of a mistake once the missiles were in place.
The Soviets also express some skepticism: The problem is compounded by a certain misunderstanding that arises when the American term "crisis management" (which is often used interchangeably with "crisis control") is translated into Russian. The Russian equivalent *(krizisnoe upravlenie)* carries a definite connotation of manipulation of a crisis to achieve unilateral foreign policy aims. Hence, American and Russian specialists discussing the topic of crisis management have often had a "dialogue of the deaf" in which the Soviets reacted strongly to a term that has neutral connotations in English.

136 "safeguards against any inadvertent use"; "that regional conflicts": *New York Times,* 15 February 1984, pp. A-1, 6.
On March 2, 1984; "making them mandatory"; "to consider the prevention"; "not to allow"; "if such a danger": *Current Digest of the Soviet Press* 36, no. 9 (28 March 1984); in a similar vein, Brezhnev raised the possibility in 1981 of instituting codes of conduct to regulate East-West competition.

137 In 1981 Senator Sam Nunn: *Congressional Record of the 97th Congress* 128, no. 46 (Monday, 26 April 1982): S3963.

138 Secretary of Defense Weinberger responded: "Report to the Congress by Secretary of Defense Caspar W. Weinberger on

PAGE

Direct Communications Links and Other Measures to Enhance Stability," 11 April 1983.

Meanwhile, the Nunn-Warner center resolution: Senate Resolution 329 "Relating to Nuclear Risk Reduction Centers," *Congressional Record of the 98th Congress* 130, no. 8 (Wednesday, 1 February 1984).

10. Making Crisis Control a Reality: Lessons from the Hotline

142 "discovered nobody quite knew": Webster A. Stone, *Hot-Line: The Origin, Development, Negotiation and Ramifications of the Direct Communications Link Between the United States and the Soviet Union,* unpublished undergraduate honors thesis, Harvard University, 1984, p, 15.

143–44 "Why aren't the president and the premier"; "Must a world be lost"; "Washington is ideologically close enough": Jess Gorkin, "Hotline to Moscow," *I Can Tell It Now* (New York: E. P. Dutton, 1964), pp. 3–5.

144 "We cannot afford to close": *Parade,* 30 October 1960, p. 60.

"It is vitally important": Ibid.

"I grabbed his hand and kept pumping it": personal communication to the author.

'I am in favor of': Jess Gorkin, "Hotline to Moscow," *I Can Tell It Now,* p. 5.

145 "Tenacious and persistent": Stone, *Hot-Line,* p. 26.

147 "One of the fellows in the office": Jess Gorkin, interview with the author, 19 November 1983.

Conclusion

156 "The football thing is cute": Donald Trump quoted in *New York Times Magazine,* 8 April 1984, p. 79.

Index